C000153245

Contents

St. Peter's Primary School
Wymondham

List of resources   3
Introduction   4
How to use the CD-ROM   5

Victorian Britain   PAGE 7
Notes on the CD-ROM resources   8
Notes on the photocopiable pages   19
Photocopiable pages   24

Victorian local history   PAGE 36
Notes on the CD-ROM resources   37
Notes on the photocopiable pages   44
Photocopiable pages   46

Britain since 1948   PAGE 52
Notes on the CD-ROM resources   53
Notes on the photocopiable pages   67
Photocopiable pages   72

Text © Pat Hoodless
© 2003 Scholastic Ltd

Published by Scholastic Ltd, Villiers House,
Clarendon Avenue, Leamington Spa,
Warwickshire CV32 5PR

Printed by Bell & Bain Ltd, Glasgow

3 4 5 6 7 8 9   5 6 7 8 9 0 1 2

British Library Cataloguing-in-Publication Data
A catalogue record for this book is available from
the British Library.

ISBN 0-439-98453-X

**Visit our website at
www.scholastic.co.uk**

CD Developed in association with
Footmark Media Ltd

Author
Pat Hoodless

Editor
Roanne Charles

Assistant Editors
Clare Gallaher and Nina Bruges

Series Designer
Joy Monkhouse

Designer
Micky Pledge

Cover photographs
© Photodisc, © Mary Evans Picture
Library, © Illustrated London News,
© National Museum of Photography,
Film & Television/Science & Society
Picture Library

Acknowledgements

The publishers wish to thank:
HarperCollins Publishers for an extract from *Windrush: The Irresistible Rise of Multi-Racial Britain* by Mike Phillips and Trevor Phillips © 1999, Mike Phillips and Trevor Phillips (1999, HarperCollins); **Oxford University Press** for the use of an extract from *Lark Rise* by Flora Thompson © 1939, Flora Thompson (1939, OUP); **Jack Hogbin** and **Mota Singh** for their involvement with the interviews.

Every effort has been made to trace copyright holders and the publishers apologise for any omissions.

Every effort has been made to ensure that websites and addresses referred to in this book are correct and educationally sound. They are believed to be correct at the time of publication. The publishers cannot be held responsible for subsequent changes in the address of a website, nor for the content of the sites mentioned. Referral to a website is not an endorsement by the publisher of that site.

Made with Macromedia is a
trademark of Macromedia, Inc.
Director ®
Copyright © 1984-2000
Macromedia, Inc.

QuickTime and the QuickTime
logo are trademarks used under
license. The QuickTime logo is
registered in the US and other
countries.

List of resources on the CD-ROM

The page numbers refer to the teacher's notes provided in this book.

Victorian Britain

Young Queen Victoria	8
Victoria and Albert	8
Victoria and great-grandchildren	9
Child labour in a mine	9
Inside a mine	10
Child labour in a mill	11
Shoeshine boy	11
A slum	12
Soup kitchen	12
Lord Shaftesbury	13
Dr Barnardo	13
Barnardo Boys	14
Barnardo's Village Home	14
Typewriting class	15
ICT lesson	15
Playing marbles	16
Playing with a hoop	16
Sliding on the ice	16
Learning to cook	17
Pegging out washing	17
Reading at home	17
Canoeing	18
Skateboarding	18

Victorian local history

Horse-drawn carriage	37
Steam train	37
Railway station	38
Paddle steamer	39
Ocean liner being built	40
Colliery	40
Textile mill	41
Terraced houses	42
Town hall	43

Britain since 1948

The British Empire in 1901	53
The Commonwealth in 2003	53
1940s suit	54
1950s flower-print dress	54
1960s mini-dress	54
1970s flared jeans	55
1980s dungarees	55
1940s telephone	56
1960s telephone	57
Mobile phone	57
Early computer	58
Laptop computer	59
The Empire Windrush	60
Immigrants from the Caribbean	60
Immigrants from Kenya	61
British passport holder	61
Interview: Immigration	62
Notting Hill Carnival in the 1970s	63
Modern Notting Hill Carnival	63
Lunar astronaut	64
Space shuttle	65
Hubble Space Telescope	65
Interview: How life has changed since 1948	66

INTRODUCTION

This book and CD-ROM support the teaching and learning set out in the QCA Scheme of Work for history in Years 5 and 6. The CD provides a large bank of varied visual resources. The book provides teacher's notes, background information, ideas for discussion and activities to accompany the CD resources, along with photocopiable pages to support teaching and learning. All have been specially chosen to meet the requirements outlined in the QCA units on Victorian Britain, Victorian local history and Britain since 1948. Additional resources and ideas have also been included to enable teachers to broaden these areas of study if they wish, such as stories, extracts from interviews, statistics and personal comments. The resources are also relevant and useful to those not necessarily following the QCA Schemes of Work, particularly teachers in Scotland.

The resources and activities are not intended to be used rigidly, however, since they do not provide a structure for teaching in themselves. The teacher's notes provide ideas for discussion and activities that focus on the 'Knowledge, skills and understanding' of the National Curriculum for history. They aim to guide teachers in developing the skills and concepts that are fundamental to children's understanding of what it is to learn about the past.

In this book, there is an emphasis on developing children's awareness and understanding of chronology, of asking and answering questions, and of investigating historical sources and communicating findings in a variety of ways. Above all, the activities and discussions aim to build clear links between the first-hand experience they gain from using the resources on the CD and their developing awareness of the past.

Links with other subjects
Research skills
Independent enquiry and the development of research skills are important in this book. Often, the activities are based on children's use of reference books, fiction and non-fiction sources and the Internet to gather further information related to a topic or individual. Work of this kind will help foster an independent, enquiring attitude on the part of the children, helping them to become more effective learners, genuinely interested in broadening their knowledge of people and events. For example, in searching the Internet for information about child labour, children will develop more detailed knowledge of conditions while improving their research skills. Through examining the images provided on the CD, children will naturally become involved in the technique of raising questions and then working to find the answers.

Literacy
There are close links between the topics covered in this book and work on literacy. Discussion activities contribute directly to the requirements for speaking and listening, as do drama and role-play activities. The stories, descriptions and accounts provide models of different genres and may be used in shared reading during the Literacy Hour or to provide a stimulus for shared, guided or independent writing. There is considerable opportunity for the children to develop their creative writing skills in the form of historical stories or information texts. Images from the CD could be printed to stimulate independent writing or to illustrate it. They may also be used to illustrate the timelines or sequence lines created in the course of each topic.

Geography
In learning about local history and the background to Commonwealth and immigration, geographical links are indispensable. Consequently, there is some emphasis on the use and interpretation of maps. Skills in reading and interpreting maps, therefore, are specifically involved in the discussion and activity points for each chapter.

ICT
Finally, there are clear links with information technology. ICT is constantly useful throughout these activities, particularly in terms of providing an inexhaustible resource for children to use in carrying out research into specific aspects of each topic. There are also opportunities for children to communicate their findings through the use of ICT in the use of word-processing and data presentation software.

HOW TO USE THE CD-ROM

Windows NT users

If you use Windows NT you may see the following error message: 'The procedure entry point Process32First could not be located in the dynamic link library KERNEL32.dll'. Click on **OK** and the CD will autorun with no further problems.

Setting up your computer for optimal use

On opening, the CD will alert you if changes are needed in order to operate the CD at its optimal use. There are three changes you may be advised to make:

Viewing resources at their maximum screen size

To see images at their maximum screen size, your screen display needs to be set to 800 x 600 pixels. In order to adjust your screen size you will need to **Quit** the program.

If using a PC, open the **Control Panel**. Select **Display** and then **Settings**. Adjust the **Desktop Area** to 800 x 600 pixels. Click on **OK** and then restart the program.

If using a Mac, from the **Apple** menu select **Control Panels** and then **Monitors** to adjust the screen size.

Adobe Acrobat Reader

To print high-quality versions of images and to view and print the photocopiable pages on the CD you need **Adobe Acrobat Reader** installed on your computer. If you do not have it installed already, a version is provided on the CD. To install this version **Quit** the 'Ready Resources' program.

If using a PC, right-click on the **Start** menu on your desktop and choose **Explore**. Click on the **+** sign to the left of the CD drive entitled 'Ready Resources' and open the folder called 'Acrobat Reader Installer'. Run the program contained in this folder to install **Adobe Acrobat Reader**.

If using a Mac, double click on the 'Ready Resources' icon on the desktop and on the 'Acrobat Reader Installer' folder. Run the program contained in this folder to install **Adobe Acrobat Reader**.

PLEASE NOTE: If you do not have **Adobe Acrobat Reader** installed, you will not be able to print high-quality versions of images, or to view or print photocopiable pages (although these are provided in the accompanying book and can be photocopied).

QuickTime

In order to view the videos and listen to the audio on this CD you will need to have **QuickTime version 5 or later** installed on your computer. If you do not have it installed already, or have an older version of **QuickTime**, the latest version is provided on the CD. If you choose to install this version, **Quit** the 'Ready Resources' program.

If using a PC, right-click on the **Start** menu on your desktop and choose **Explore**. Click on the **+** sign to the left of the CD drive that is entitled 'Ready Resources' and open the folder called 'QuickTime Installer'. Run the program contained in this folder to install **QuickTime**.

If using a Mac, double click on the 'Ready Resources' CD icon on the desktop and then on the 'Acrobat Reader Installer' folder. Run the program contained in this folder to install **QuickTime**.

PLEASE NOTE: If you do not have **QuickTime** installed you will be unable to view the films.

Menu screen

▶ Click on the **Resource Gallery** of your choice to view the resources available under that topic.
▶ Click on **Complete Resource Gallery** to view all the resources available on the CD.
▶ Click on **Photocopiable Resources (PDF format)** to view a list of the photocopiables provided in the book that accompanies this CD.
▶ **Back**: click to return to the **opening screen**. Click **Continue** to move to the **Menu screen**.
▶ **Quit**: click **Quit** to close the menu program and progress to the **Quit screen.** If you quit from the **Quit screen** you will exit the CD. If you do not quit you will return to the **Menu screen**.

Resource Galleries

▶ **Help**: click **Help** to find support on accessing and using images.
▶ **Back to menu:** click here to return to the **Menu screen**.
▶ **Quit:** click here to move to the **Quit screen** – see **Quit** above.

Viewing images

Small versions of each image are shown in the Resource Gallery. Click and drag the slider on the slide bar to scroll through the images in the Resource Gallery, or click on the arrows to move the images frame by frame. Roll the pointer over an image to see the caption.

▶ Click on an image to view the screen-sized version of it.

▶ To return to the Resource Gallery click on **Back to Resource Gallery**.

Viewing videos

Click on the video icon of your choice in the Resource Gallery. In order to view the videos on this CD, you will need to have **QuickTime** installed on your computer (see 'Setting up your computer for optimal use' above).

Once at the video screen, use the buttons on the bottom of the video screen to operate the video. The slide bar can be used for a fast forward and rewind. To return to the Resource Gallery click on **Back to Resource Gallery**.

Listening to sound recordings

Click on the required sound icon. Use the buttons or the slide bar to hear the sound. A transcript will be displayed on the viewing screen where appropriate. To return to the Resource Gallery, click on **Back to Resource Gallery**.

Printing

Click on the image to view it (see 'Viewing images' above). There are two print options:

Print using Acrobat enables you to print a high-quality version of an image. Choosing this option means that the image will open as a read-only page in **Adobe Acrobat** and in order to access these files you will need to have already installed **Adobe Acrobat Reader** on your computer (see 'Setting up your computer for optimal use' above). To print the selected resource, select **File** and then **Print**. Once you have printed the resource **minimise** or **close** the Adobe screen using — or **X** in the top right-hand corner of the screen. Return to the Resource Gallery by clicking on **Back to Resource Gallery**.

Simple print enables you to print a lower quality version of the image without the need to use **Adobe Acrobat Reader**. Select the image and click on the **Simple print** option. After printing, click on **Back to Resource Gallery**.

Slideshow presentation

If you would like to present a number of resources without having to return to the Resource Gallery and select a new image each time, you can compile a slideshow. Click on the **+** tabs at the top of each image in the Resource Gallery you would like to include in your presentation (pictures, sound and video can be included). It is important that you click on the images in the order in which you would like to view them (a number will appear on each tab to confirm the order). If you would like to change the order, click on **Clear slideshow** and begin again. Once you have selected your images – up to a maximum of 20 – click on **Play slideshow** and you will be presented with the first of your selected resources. To move to the next selection in your slideshow click on **Next slide**, to see a previous resource click on **Previous slide**. You can end your slideshow presentation at any time by clicking on **Resource Gallery**. Your slideshow selection will remain selected until you **Clear slideshow** or return to the **Menu screen**.

Viewing on an interactive whiteboard or data projector

Resources can be viewed directly from the CD. To make viewing easier for a whole class, use a large monitor, data projector or interactive whiteboard. For group, paired or individual work, the resources can be viewed from the computer screen.

Photocopiable resources (PDF format)

To view or print a photocopiable resource page, click on the required title in the list and the page will open as a read-only page in **Adobe Acrobat**. In order to access these files you will need to have already installed **Adobe Acrobat Reader** on your computer (see 'Setting up your computer for optimal use' above). To print the selected resource select **File** and then **Print**. Once you have printed the resource **minimise** or **close** the Adobe screen using — or **X** in the top right-hand corner of the screen. This will take you back to the list of PDF files. To return to the **Menu screen**, click on **Back**.

VICTORIAN BRITAIN

Content, skills and concepts

This chapter relates to unit 11 of the QCA Scheme of Work and will assist in planning and resourcing work on Victorian Britain. It is assumed that this unit will be taught mainly to Year 5 or 6, and that it may also be adapted for earlier age groups. This chapter introduces the characteristic features of the lives of Victorian children. It demonstrates how children lived in Victorian times, what attitudes were towards children and how these attitudes came to change.

Together with the Victorian Britain Resource Gallery on the CD-ROM, this chapter introduces a range of sources, including images of Victoria, illustrations of child labour, images of mills, mines and slum dwellings, reports and stories. These can be used in teaching about Victorian Britain as a country with both rich and very poor people. The chapter also provides materials to support the teaching of key historical concepts relevant to this period and theme.

Children will already have gained experience of sequencing and using timelines, using time-related vocabulary, asking and answering questions, and using written, visual and auditory sources. Recounting stories about the past, and looking for similarities and differences between the past and the present are prior learning activities that will have introduced relevant skills and concepts to the children before they progress to the skills and concepts in this unit. This chapter includes suggestions for the extension of these and other skills, such as recognising change and continuity and the ability to select and use information to support an argument.

Resources on the CD-ROM

Images of key individuals, rich and poor children, homes, workplaces, school and leisure pursuits are provided on the CD-ROM. Background information about these sources is provided in the teacher's notes, along with ideas for further work on them.

Photocopiable pages

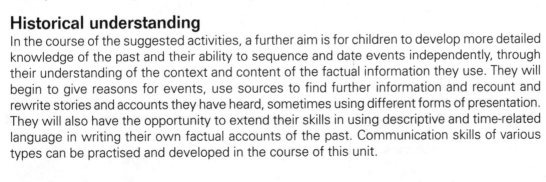

Photocopiable resources at the end of the chapter (and also in PDF format on the CD) include:
- ▶ word cards that highlight the essential vocabulary of this topic
- ▶ a timeline
- ▶ brief biographies of Lord Shaftesbury and Dr Barnardo
- ▶ fiction and non-fiction pieces on Victorian schools, workplaces and leisure.

The teacher's notes that accompany the photocopiable pages include suggestions for developing discussion and for using them as whole class, group or individual activities. Within the photocopiable texts, topic-specific vocabulary is introduced. Fiction extracts highlight differences between life now and then, as well as the discrepancies between the lives of the rich and those of ordinary Victorians. The texts can be used for shared or guided reading, and more able children could read some of them independently.

History skills

Skills such as observation, description, the use of time-related vocabulary, sequencing, using a timeline, understanding the meaning of dates, comparing, inferring, listening, speaking, reading, writing and drawing are all involved in the activities suggested. For example, there is an opportunity to develop independent sequencing skills through the use of a timeline to which children can add additional information as they discover it. Children can learn to use descriptive vocabulary to discuss the images provided on the CD.

Historical understanding

In the course of the suggested activities, a further aim is for children to develop more detailed knowledge of the past and their ability to sequence and date events independently, through their understanding of the context and content of the factual information they use. They will begin to give reasons for events, use sources to find further information and recount and rewrite stories and accounts they have heard, sometimes using different forms of presentation. They will also have the opportunity to extend their skills in using descriptive and time-related language in writing their own factual accounts of the past. Communication skills of various types can be practised and developed in the course of this unit.

NOTES ON THE CD-ROM RESOURCES

Young Queen Victoria

Queen Victoria is shown here as a young queen, one year after her accession to the throne. She came to the throne in 1837 at the age of 18, after the death of her uncle, King William IV. Ruling over one of the largest empires the world has ever known must have been a daunting task for such a young person. However, Victoria is portrayed here as calm, charming, serene and regal. The portrait has clearly been made with the intention of presenting her as an authoritative royal figure. Indeed, Victoria was to have many portraits and photographs made with this very intention, in an attempt to bolster the popularity of the monarchy at a time when it had sunk quite low in the public esteem.

Victoria and Albert

This artist's impression shows Victoria at her wedding in 1840 to Albert, Prince of Saxe-Coburg-Gotha in Germany. The wedding was held in the Chapel Royal in St James's Palace, and Victoria describes it in her diary as 'imposing, and fine and simple'. Their marriage and family life were held up as a model for the rest of the country, and numerous portraits were subsequently made showing the couple with their family. Victoria was genuinely devoted to Albert and they had nine children. Albert was able to take on much of the burden of managing government, ministers and advisers, and was responsible for several initiatives, such as the design of the Crystal Palace, built for the Great Exhibition of 1851. Following his somewhat premature death from typhoid in 1861, Victoria was thrown into deep despair. She went into mourning for her 'dearest Albert' and remained so until her death in 1901.

Discussing the pictures

▶ Look at the two images of the young Queen Victoria and ask the children to identify what kind of pictures they are, and how they have been made. (Both engravings.)

▶ Discuss how both of these pictures show us the queen through the eyes of an artist. Consider the implications of this. For example, the artist might want to make the queen look special or change her appearance to suit what was wanted.

▶ Discuss the portrait, and consider the impression the artist, or the subject, wanted viewers of it to gain about the queen. What does her expression tell us? What about her clothes and jewellery?

▶ Examine the etching of Victoria's wedding, and discuss again what impression the artist wishes to convey.

▶ Compare how the portrait gives quite a formal impression, while the wedding scene looks quite informal. Talk about why this may have been. Perhaps the wedding was quite informal; there are more things going on in that picture; it is an image of a scene, a moment, rather than someone who would have sat for her portrait.

▶ How might we tell from the picture that it is an important wedding? For example, the attire of the bride and groom and that of the others present.

Activities

▶ Refer to the timeline on photocopiable page 28 and remind the children of the dates of Queen Victoria's reign. Ask the children to identify the dates of her jubilees. Locate and label the date of her wedding to Albert on the timeline.

▶ Provide a wide range of sources for the children to use independently, and set them the task of finding out about Victoria's early life, her accession to the throne, her marriage and her children. Ask them to find out more about Albert too. You could put the children into groups and allocate them one aspect each. By narrowing the focus of their research, the information found will be more detailed. Sources could include extracts from Victoria's own journal (published by Penguin, for example, in *Queen Victoria in Her Letters and Journal* edited by Christopher Hibbert).

▶ Ask the children to write a detailed description of one of the pictures. They may need to look up the special names of some of the royal regalia or parts of the chapel.

▶ Take the hot-seat in the role of the young queen and let the children ask you about how she would have felt when she became queen and at her wedding.

Victoria and great-grandchildren

In this photograph we see Victoria towards the end of her life, in 1900. By this time, she had a number of grandchildren and great-grandchildren. The children in this photograph are the children of the Duke and Duchess of York (later King George V and Queen Mary) and are Victoria's great-grandchildren. They are: Prince Albert (later King George VI – George was the name chosen by the new king, as traditional in the royal family) sitting on the cushion, with Princess Victoria behind him, next to her is Prince Edward (later King Edward VIII) and the baby is Prince Henry.

What is significant from this photograph is the lifestyle these children were accustomed to. They were well fed, well clothed and pampered. Their every need was likely to have been catered for by several servants. Prince Henry is lavishly dressed. The family is posed on a ground mat and there are soft cushions available. The children appear well groomed, well cared for and confident. The queen, encouraged to emerge from the somewhat reclusive existence she took following Albert's death, poses for a family portrait, again with the intention of revealing something of the monarchy's family life and setting an example to her people. Victoria was the first British monarch to be photographed, and was a great supporter of the technology.

Discussing the photograph

▶ Ask the children who they think is shown in this photograph.

▶ Discuss the surroundings in which the picture is set. For example, the large gardens or parklands and the trappings of comfort.

▶ Look at the children's clothes and at how they are posing for the picture. Discuss what impression this gives of them.

▶ Look closely at the queen and the care with which she is holding the baby. Talk about how she might have felt at having such a new great-grandchild.

▶ Compare how the baby is dressed with the clothes worn by modern babies.

▶ Think about how the status of this family is conveyed in the picture.

▶ Discuss possible reasons why the photograph was taken.

Activities

▶ Ask the children to write a description of the photograph, adding comments on the impression it gives of the queen and her family.

▶ Ask the children to research Victoria's family, from her ancestors to her own children grandchildren and great-grandchildren. Demonstrate how to draw a family tree and a simple time chart and ask the children to compile these with the information they find.

▶ Find other examples of family photographs of Victoria and make a class 'Victorian family album'.

▶ Read the extract from *Lark Rise* on photocopiable page 35, and discuss how the monarchy was so popular by this stage that these jubilee celebrations were held across the country.

Child labour in a mine

By stark comparison with the royal children above, poor children at the beginning of Victoria's reign were subjected to the harshest of living and working conditions. This illustration was drawn for the commission set up to investigate working conditions in mines in 1842. The children shown are quite small, necessarily so, since the tunnel they work in is also very small. Their labour was very heavy, involving pushing and pulling heavy trucks full of coal up to the surface in seams that were too narrow and low for pit ponies to work. The hours of work would have been extremely long, probably in excess of 12 hours a day, and the children were paid by the number of trucks they moved. Working conditions were brutish, and the children received no education. Not everyone, however, was prepared to tolerate these conditions and many influential people began to campaign against these outrages, such as Lord Shaftesbury (see page 13 and photocopiable page 31).

Discussing the picture

▶ Ask the children what they think is shown in this engraving. Where do they think it is set?

▶ Discuss the likely ages of the figures shown in it. Tell the class that children as young as six or seven were sometimes employed.

▶ Look at what they are doing and explain to the children about child labour in the mines.
▶ Why do they think that small children were made to do work like this?
▶ Discuss any other reasons there may have been for making children work. (To bring in more money for the family.)
▶ Talk about attitudes to childhood at this time, and explain that children from poor families were expected to work as soon as they could. Consider the implications of this for the children. (For example, they were not educated; they often suffered injuries and illness.)
▶ Ask the children if they think that the children of the rich worked hard like this.
▶ Ask them if they would like to work in a mine.

Activities
See 'Inside a mine', below.

Inside a mine

This contemporary engraving shows the large cavernous area at the bottom of a mine shaft in Newcastle, in about 1860. Large 'galleries' would have branched off around this area, where more mining for coal would take place. What is particularly notable from this image is the large number of children, including girls, working in the mine. Some carry lanterns, some dress ore (sort the useful ore from 'waste' rock), while others sit, perhaps exhausted, on the ground.

Mining of both coal and slate was very labour-intensive in the 19th century and children were useful in a number of ways. They could be paid less than adults, thereby increasing the mine owner's profits, and they could get into small spaces, meaning that smaller seams could be worked, extracting every possible piece of coal from the area. (See 'Child labour in a mine', above.) The conditions in the mines would be very cold, damp, dark, dusty and often cramped, resulting in ill health for much of the workers' lives, especially from the coal dust, which caused lung disease. There were also risks of being hurt by falling rocks, especially during blasting, being hit by the trucks on the railway lines, or injury from tools while working.

Discussing the picture
▶ Ask the children what they think this engraving shows.
▶ Look at the size of this cavern and ask the children to imagine how cold and damp it would have been to work in.
▶ Talk about the dust and smell in the mine, perhaps using some real coal for the children to see what it is like.
▶ Look at the people in the mine, suggesting how many are children.
▶ Establish what the children are doing and how they look. (Some look ill or exhausted.)
▶ Think about the dangers of working in a place like this.
▶ Explain how other galleries would lead off from this place, with tunnels going into the coal seams in different directions.
▶ If anyone has been into a mine, ask them to describe their impressions of the place.

Activities
▶ Find out about other work children did in the 19th century (see 'Shoeshine boy' and 'Child labour in a mill' on the CD), and ask the children to make a wall display, adding their own captions and descriptions.
▶ If possible, take the children to visit the site of an old mine, to learn about conditions at first hand.
▶ Provide information about the working of mines in the 19th century, for the children to make notes about the equipment used and the jobs that had to be done.
▶ Ask the children to research further specifically into child labour in the mines. Organise the class into groups, one member of each in the role of an interviewer. Tell the interviewers to ask the rest of the children, in role as mine workers, about the conditions, food, work and pay that they received. Tape the interviews.
▶ Challenge the children to write an imaginary story based on a day in the life of a child working in a mine.
▶ Encourage the children to find out about Lord Shaftesbury's efforts into improving standards of living for children (see page 13 and photocopiable page 31) and other philanthropists of the time, such as Edwin Chadwick.

Child labour in a mill

This is a photograph of a girl working in a cotton mill. Many children were employed in the textile industry, as they were cheap to employ, they were quick and small, and could also be used to get into difficult places in the machinery to mend broken threads or to clean out dust. Here, this girl is checking the smooth running of the threads on a power loom. This was a skilled job, since great accuracy and speed were required to spot and fix any damage without affecting production or stopping the machinery. Children were expected to run and work deftly and quickly to keep machinery working, and their pay would be cut if they were deemed responsible for any losses in production. Very often there were terrible accidents, where a child would be caught in the moving machinery. They also often worked as long as 12 hours a day with only one break of an hour, and tiredness could lead to further accidents.

Discussing the photograph

▶ Ask the children if they have ever seen a place like this before and if anyone can work out what it is.

▶ See if the children know what took place inside textile mills like this, and talk about the different kinds of mill there are. Explain that this is a textile mill, where spinning and weaving of cloth takes place.

▶ How old do the children think the girl in this picture is? (She could be as young as eight.)

▶ Discuss why she is at work and not in school. (She needed to work to help support her family. Education was the preserve of the wealthy and not considered important for all children.)

▶ Discuss what it conditions in the mill were like: very noisy, very dusty, very tiring.

▶ Explain about the dangers of working amongst moving machinery, and how accidents were frequent.

Activities

▶ Let children search suitable sites on the Internet for further information about the lives of people who worked in the mills. They could also refer to the mill rules (see photocopiable page 30) to see how closely regulated the lives of the workers were and the unreasonable demands that were placed on them.

▶ Working with the whole class, create a short drama about an accident in the mill. Create a playscript during a shared writing session and then provide time for the children to practise a performance. You could get some ideas from Scholastic's Performance Play *Whistle as You Walk Away*.

▶ Ask the children to use the information they have found out about working in the mills to write 'a day in the life' of a child working in a mill. How does this compare with their own average day? Encourage them to look at the 'Biography of Lord Shaftesbury' on photocopiable page 31, which includes details of the working hours of some child workers.

▶ Read the extract from *North and South* by Elizabeth Gaskell on photocopiable page 29. Ask the children to write a report of Bessie's illness and its causes in their own words.

Shoeshine boy

This little boy is not more than six or seven years old. However, he is working industriously at his trade as a shoeshine boy. He has his tools set out in an organised way and his coat and hat neatly hung up. He has swept up his area and has found a useful basket to use as his workbench. From his own clothes, it is possible to see that he is very poor. His coat is old, worn and dusty. His own boots are worn out, probably hand-me-downs as they don't seem to fit him properly, and he has only just enough lacing to keep them on his feet.

Many young children had to work like this, bootblacking or selling newspapers, any occupation that would bring in extra money to keep their families, or themselves if they were orphans. Until the Education Acts of 1881 and 1891, it was not generally accepted that education was an expectation for all children, and many did not receive any, or would only have attended Sunday School where they received rudimentary instruction in reading, writing, arithmetic and Bible study.

Discussing the photograph

▶ Look carefully at this picture with the children, and discuss what kind of picture it is. Note that, being a photograph, it must come from the later Victorian period.

- Discuss the age of the little boy. Compare his size with the size of the boots he is cleaning.
- Find volunteers to describe his attitude to his work and the evidence for this.
- Discuss whether he is very poor and what the clues are that tell us. Consider whether this child is likely to have earned enough money to feed himself well. Mention that malnutrition and lack of food were often a danger to children like these.
- Notice how his workplace is essentially portable, and consider what he could try to do if he could not find enough customers in one area.
- Explain how attitudes to children and childhood were different in Victorian times. Children were expected to work like everyone else; they were not expected to express, or even have, their own opinions; they could only do what they were told because they were not considered to have any rights.
- Ask the children if they would have liked to live in times when adults had that attitude. Perhaps they would like to be more independent than they are now, but perhaps there are problems with having to be independent at too young an age.

Activities
- Ask the children to carry out their own enquiries into everyday life in Victorian England, particularly to find out what kind of jobs were done by the very poor in society. Make a list of the jobs found, then allocate each type of work to a different group to extend the research.
- Talk about the fact that many children worked so that they and their families earned enough to avoid ending up in the workhouse. Ask the children to find out about workhouses. Do they think that they would rather work than live in a workhouse, if they could get jobs?
- Provide opportunities for groups of children to act out short dramas based on their understanding of the lives of child workers.
- Challenge the children to write a short piece about the things that a boy like the one in the photograph could do if he did not get enough customers. Ask them to include the possible consequences of any actions he might take, for example if he decided to try to steal something.

A slum

This is a contemporary cartoon drawn by George Cruikshank, otherwise known as 'Boz'. Boz often illustrated the works of Charles Dickens, many of which recounted the horrors of life for the poor, particularly in the large cities of Victorian England. This cartoon, from about 1836, shows street life in Monmouth Street in the Seven Dials area of London. Cruikshank vividly presents the overcrowded, squalid conditions that the poor lived in. What stands out is the lack of amenities, particularly for the children, who lived and played in the street. Here they play in the waste water flowing down the gutter, 'fishing' and sailing boats in it. The danger of infection and disease are very apparent. Outbreaks of cholera and typhoid were not that uncommon.

Soup kitchen

During the early part of the reign of Queen Victoria, thousands of people moved from the countryside to find work and a better life in the rapidly industrialised towns and cities. Very often they were not successful, and were unable to find jobs or places to live. As a result, huge slums developed, where people found a place to sleep wherever they could, such as in damp, unhealthy cellars. Many thousands of people lived in overcrowded houses in streets full of rubbish and over a third of the population of England earned less than a living wage. Christian groups began to work to help these starving, impoverished people, among them the Salvation Army. Churches and chapels set up soup kitchens to provide the needy with at least some basic food, and people were provided with shelter when possible. The need for such drastic action highlights the severity of the situation, which the government of the time did not consider its responsibility.

Discussing the pictures
- Ask the children what they think is going on in these pictures.
- Explain the meaning of the word *slum* and tell the children that the first picture shows a commercial street in a slum.
- Point out the crowding and the lack of amenities.
- Discuss the games the children are playing and the problems of where they are playing.

▶ Tell the children about the function of political cartoons and suggest that Cruikshank, conscious of his audience, may have exaggerated some of the features to make a point. Nevertheless, we can still use the picture to gain some information about this aspect of Victorian life.

▶ Explain that the second picture is an engraving of a scene showing a busy soup kitchen. Ask the children if they have ever heard the term before and know what it means.

▶ Discuss why soup kitchens were needed, referring to 'A slum' where necessary.

▶ Explain that it was very often people in the churches or groups like the Salvation Army, concerned about what they saw, who set up these places to try to help people and prevent them from starving.

▶ Look at the vast number of people in the soup kitchen, and tell the children how widespread poverty was in many parts of Britain, particularly the large cities, where people had gone in search of work and where slums grew up.

▶ Discuss how the soup seems to have been made (in huge vats), and what it was probably like to eat.

▶ Encourage the children to imagine what it must have felt like to be a child waiting in such a huge crowd for some soup. Some of the children (especially orphans) would have gone on their own. Look at the faces of the women dishing out the soup and discuss how friendly and sympathetic they appear to be.

Activities

▶ Remind the children that the Salvation Army set up many of the soup kitchens. Discuss the meaning of the word *salvation*, and get the children to find out further information about the organisation and its work.

▶ Tell the children that in Victorian times, people who remained very poor or could not look after themselves, became inmates of workhouses. Challenge the children to work in pairs to find out and make notes about workhouses.

▶ Read the extract from Chapter 2 of Dickens' *Oliver Twist*, where Oliver asks the workhouse master for more gruel. Compare this incident with the likely reaction a child would have had if they had done the same in the soup kitchen shown in this picture.

▶ Divide the class into three or four groups and advise them they have a budget of less than one pound. Tell them they must devise a recipe for soup that will cost no more than this to make. Alternatively, they could find a recipe for, and make, some thin gruel (a kind of watery porridge).

Lord Shaftesbury

This photograph of Anthony Ashley Cooper, who became Lord Ashley, Earl of Shaftesbury, was taken in 1870. From a religious family in the aristocracy, he led a privileged life, attending boarding school and then studying at Oxford University. As an MP, he learned about the lives of the poor, and of poor children in particular, and resolved to try his best to improve their situations. In 1832, he became leader of the Factory Reform Movement and actively campaigned in Parliament. Lord Shaftesbury found this role a frustrating one at times, and critics would say that his factory reform campaigning was generated 'as much from a dislike of the mill owners as sympathy with the mill workers'. His commission's 1842 report on mines and collieries was groundbreaking, as many people in the country were unaware that there were women and children miners.

This posed photograph reflects the kind of character Lord Shaftesbury was, a well brought up Victorian, refined, thoughtful and highly educated. It clearly shows that he was a member of the privileged classes.

Dr Barnardo

Dr Thomas Barnardo was a similar kind of philanthropist to Lord Shaftesbury, but, with a different role in society, he adopted different methods to address the problems of the poor. He adopted evangelical Christianity and preached for a while, before he moved to London to study medicine. He didn't gain medical qualifications, but became known as 'Dr'.

Barnardo was horrified by the living conditions of many children in the city. He was a powerful and emotive speaker and, while giving a talk about the children's problems, he was heard by Lord Shaftesbury and Robert Barclay, and both men were so moved that they agreed to support him in his wish to help these children. He was then able to set up homes for orphaned and destitute boys and girls. His homes continued to provide care well into the 20th century.

The 'pose' in this photograph reflects Dr Barnardo's character. He was an educated, very hard working man, who appears determined and concerned about the tasks he wanted to accomplish. His dress and appearance show that he was a middle-class professional person.

Discussing the photographs

▶ Look at the two photographs and explain that the first shows Lord Shaftesbury and the second Dr Barnado.

▶ See if any of the children has heard of these people before, and establish what they already know. Then tell the class more about the work of the two men.

▶ Ask the children if they can see significant differences between the two men. Let them know, for example, that one came form a wealthy background, and one from an ordinary background. Discuss if they might be able to tell this from the pictures.

▶ Look at the activities the men are engaged in and consider why these pictures were taken. (For example, to present them as hard-working, educated men, to promote their work.) The portait of Lord Shaftesbury certainly seems to have been specially posed for, whereas the photograph of Dr Barnardo could have been taken while he was genuinely busy at work, or he might have posed to give this impression.

▶ Briefly review some of the work they did towards ameliorating the lives of poor children in Victorian times.

Activities

▶ Provide a wide range of resources for the children to search for more information about Shaftesbury and Barnardo.

▶ Read the brief outlines of their activities (see photocopiable pages 31 and 32) and discuss the influence the men had that has meant they are still remembered today.

▶ Set the children the task of writing a biography for one of the men.

▶ Challenge them to find out about an influential Victorian woman, such as Elizabeth Fry, Elizabeth Gaskell or Florence Nightingale, and to write her biography.

Barnardo boys

It was the sight of groups of children such as the ones in this photograph that prompted Dr Barnardo to give speeches and raise money to establish children's homes. Many children in Britain's cities lived on the streets; homeless, sometimes orphaned and having to make for themselves whatever living they could, often falling into crime.

In this photograph, they look dirty, tired, hungry and ill-clothed, some with no shoes. Such scenes inspired people of all different walks of life to act, from humble churchgoers, to those at the highest level of society. They also inspired many of the scenes and stories in the novels of Charles Dickens and Charles Kingsley. Dr Barnardo opened his first home in 1868, and by the time of his death in 1905, there were about 8000 children resident in his care homes.

Barnardo's Village Home

This Village Home for girls was set up by Dr Barnardo in Ilford, Essex. It was a small community in its own right, with its own school, laundry and church. Over 1000 girls lived there in 70 cottages. The aim of the home was that it should be like a real home for the girls and it was run on what were at the time thought to be family principles. Opened in 1876 just for girls, it accommodated both boys and girls from 1945, and then closed in 1991. It was the only Village Home he established. In this photograph, a group of girls are having tea on the lawn of one of the houses.

Discussing the photographs

▶ Look at the group of boys and remind the children about the reasons Barnardo set up his care homes.

▶ Examine the picture in more detail. Find volunteers to point out the signs that these boys are in great difficulties, such as the lack of shoes and the ragged clothing. How do the children think they may have got this way?

▶ Look at the second picture. Find volunteers to point out things that suggest these children are now better off, such as the comfortable home in the background, their being served tea.
▶ Examine the second picture. Discuss what life might have been like in a home like this. Look at the way the adults are dressed, and discuss whether this is really very homely or more formal.
▶ The benefits seem clear, but talk about possible disadvantages of children being put into large homes like this. For example, they would not have had the experience of a real home, the discipline could have been quite strict, they would have had to live with many other children, who might not always have been kind to them.

Activities

▶ Challenge the children to research further into the life and religious beliefs of Dr Barnardo (see photocopiable page 32), the homes he set up and the reasons why the homes are now closed. Ask them to make notes as they work and to use these notes to talk to the class about their findings.
▶ Ask the children to find out where the homes were and to mark these on a map.
▶ Set the task of creating a class book about Dr Barnado and his work. This could combine shared, group and independent pieces of writing.

Typewriting class

At the beginning of Victoria's reign, few children went to school. However, following the Elementary Education Act in 1870, many more schools were built and in 1880, school was made compulsory between the ages of 5 and 13, although if a child reached a certain standard earlier than 13, he or she was allowed to leave.

This photograph was taken in 1895 at Lavender Hill Board School. The girls are shown with the desks and equipment they would use in a typewriting lesson. It is interesting to note that it is only girls who were thought to need these skills, an idea that persisted for many years. At the time, the typewriter was a relatively new invention and it was beginning to be adopted in work in very much the same way as the computer in recent years. Despite the fact that there do not appear to be enough typewriters for the whole class, the school is clearly proud of this lesson, since they have had their photograph specially taken. This is also an unusually small class for a Board School – those set up by the local authority boards of education. As in all school photographs of this time, the pupils all sit and stand in the same pose and appear to be strictly disciplined. The classroom, compared with a modern day classroom, is rather bleak and bare.

Discussing the photograph

▶ Ask volunteers to explain what the picture shows.
▶ Discuss the classroom shown and how it compares with a modern classroom.
▶ Look at the expressions of the girls (and their teachers), and discuss how they may have felt about having their photograph taken.
▶ Discuss why only girls are learning to type.
▶ Talk about the attitudes towards girls and boys, and men and women in Victorian times. Discuss how they have changed in modern times.
▶ Look at the number of typewriters available, and think about how the lesson would have to be organised so that each girl could practise using one.
▶ Discuss why the school decided to have the picture taken. (Perhaps because they were proud of their new lesson; as publicity.)

Activities

See 'ICT lesson', below, for activities comparing the two photographs.

ICT lesson

Like the girls in the typewriter class from the 19th century, this photograph shows a group of girls in a modern class having a lesson in ICT. The fact that only girls are shown may be coincidence, as boys and girls are generally taught together in the present day. They are shown working in a modern computer suite, where each child in the group has access to her own computer and space around her. The room is comfortable and colourful in comparison with its 19th-century predecessor, and there is plenty of equipment available in the form of the school's software and books on shelves around the room. There is clearly an emphasis on individual work and skill development, compared with the old-fashioned typewriter lesson, where the girls will all have worked in the same way on the same piece of text.

Discussing the photograph

▶ Discuss what is happening in the picture, and think about how the children are working. For example, they seem to have different pictures on their screens, suggesting they are working creatively and fairly independently.

▶ Ask the children to compare this photograph with that of the typewriting lesson. Encourage them to notice, for example, the different way the classrooms are set out and what is visible around the girls. Discuss the implications of the different classroom layouts on the way that the teachers and children work.

Activities

▶ Read the extract from *Nicholas Nickleby* by Charles Dickens (on photocopiable page 33) to give the children more, humorous, ideas about Victorian school life.

▶ Find out more about Victorian schools, focusing on the subjects that were taught and how the lessons were given. Encourage children to find out about the equipment and layout of Victorian classrooms, making use of the word cards on photocopiable page 27 in their reports.

▶ If possible, provide an early typewriter for the children to look at and use. They can make labelled diagrams about its appearance and use.

▶ Point out the dates of some of the important inventions included on the timeline on photocopiable page 28. Then, in groups, challenge the children to research the development of the typewriter and other forms of communication in Victorian times, such as the telephone, wireless radio, the postal service, trains, steam ships, motor cars and so on.

▶ Read the 'School inspector's report' on photocopiable page 34. In conjunction with the photographs, discuss how strict and rigid everything seems in it. Ask the children to highlight the words that reflect this.

Playing marbles

Here, schoolchildren are playing a game of marbles in their break time. The photograph was taken at a school in Whitechapel, in London, in 1887. Although part of the city, it looks more like a village school to us. Marbles was a very popular game and was taken quite seriously, as can be seen in the intent expressions of the players and onlookers. Marbles were sometimes used as bottle stoppers, and when children were sent to return bottles to a shop, they would often break them to get the marble inside.

Playing with a hoop

Bowling hoops along the streets and lanes was another favourite pastime of many Victorian children. It is known to have been a popular game for thousands of years, even dating back to Egyptian times. This illustration of a boy running along beside his hoop dates from 1880.

Many simple games would be played by children in the streets, such as skipping with a long rope stretched across the street, skating, ball games, whip and top, hopscotch, and bouncing balls against the walls of the houses. Most ordinary children and those from poorer homes would expect to play in the streets whenever they were not needed to help with work in the home or in the fields, factories and mines. An interesting discussion could be had with the class about why street games like this are hardly ever played these days.

Sliding on the ice

Children in Victorian times often took great pleasure in simple pastimes. This illustration dates from about 1888, and shows children sliding round on the ice of a frozen stream or pond. Sliding and skating were popular with adults too. There are numerous accounts of accidents when people went out to skate on thin ice that gave way.

Again, it would be an interesting discussion to hold with children on why they are discouraged from sliding and skating on ice out in the open in the present day, and would contribute to the health and safety education of the children.

Discussing the pictures

▶ Look at these pictures of common pastimes and discuss who could have participated in them. Suggest they would all be activities available to any children, whether rich or poor.

▶ Discuss how, nevertheless, they were most likely to have been played by the poorer children and consider why this was. (Wealthier families could afford more sophisticated toys, their children often had more 'structured' play times and areas.)

▶ Ask the children to suggest other games that could be played by all in the street.

▶ Discuss why these games are played less often now, or not at all.

▶ Consider the safety implications of skating and sliding on frozen water.

Activities

▶ If possible, make a collection of items needed to play these old games, such as marbles, hoops, chalk for hopscotch, skipping ropes and so on, and set aside some playtimes where the children can use them. Ask them to talk about what it was like to play the games.

▶ Working with the children, make a list of the games that children play now and the modern toys they have. Alongside, list the games and toys discussed above. Compare the lists and pick out the games and toys that were popular in Victorian times and are still played with today, such as a yo-yo.

▶ Challenge the children to select two games, one old and one modern, and to write an argument about the merits of one as opposed to the other.

▶ Read the extract on photocopiable page 35 about how a special day was celebrated and the entertainments that were provided.

▶ If possible, organise a visit to a museum to look at a display of old toys and games.

Learning to cook

This illustration shows a group of children from a fairly well-to-do household, in the kitchen with their servant or cook. The children are dressed in expensive clothes. The girls have well-made dresses with lace and flowing ribbons, and ribbons in their carefully styled hair. The little boy wears a typical sailor suit, very popular with the middle classes at that time. The servant, by contrast, is dressed plainly in working clothes. The idea of mixing food in a bowl is clearly a novelty for the children and is being seen as a special treat, perhaps at Christmas time.

Pegging out washing

Taken around 1900, this photograph shows a little girl from a comfortable home pegging out her doll's washing. The girl's clothes are crumpled, but look quite new, and she has a bonnet and, for those days, very expensive toys. Apart from the dolls and their many clothes, there is also a lovely doll's pram, complete with blankets. The house has a garden area for the little girl to play in, rather than her playing in the street.

Reading at home

This late 19th century photograph shows a small boy from a very affluent background, reading in the drawing room of his home. This child is well groomed, with immaculate hair. He is smartly dressed in expensive-looking clothes and sits in an elegant chair, with a large cushion for his feet. The home is spacious, with a tall window and is luxuriously furnished with warm carpets, curtains and a picture on the wall. Framed photographs, porcelain and a vase of flowers decorate the room. The child reads his picture book with apparent interest (although this photograph would probably have been specially posed), and he has at least one other book at his disposal. Children from poor backgrounds were unlikely to see a book of this kind during their childhood, even after they had learned to read, which not all of them did.

Discussing the pictures

▶ Look at the three pictures and discuss what kind of children they show.

▶ Discuss how we can tell that they probably come from privileged homes. (The contexts, the servant, their dress.)

▶ Establish what is common about the kind of activities they are engaged in, for example that they need costly equipment; they are indoors.

▶ Compare how similar each of these activities is to present-day ones.

▶ Discuss whether poorer children would have been likely to enjoy activities like these. (Helping to cook, for example, was more likely to have been a chore than a pastime.)

Activities

▶ Compare these pictures with those of poorer children playing ('Playing marbles', 'Playing with a hoop' and 'Sliding on ice'). Discuss whether the wealthy children are likely to have played the street games, and why not. Talk about which games today's children would have enjoyed playing and why. Would they like to play with lots of other children, rather than on their own at home?

▶ Let the children carry out their own investigations of what kind of games were played by well-off children in the past.

▶ Suggest to the children that they produce a set of interview questions and ask their parents and grandparents about the games they used to play and pastimes they enjoyed when they were children. They could tape the interviews and then play the recordings to the class.

▶ Working in pairs, ask the children to make a list of all the games they can think of that can be played indoors. Challenge them to then reduce this list to include only those likely to have been played in the past. They can then justify their choices either in a discussion or in writing.

Canoeing

This photograph shows a group of modern children having a canoeing lesson. It illustrates the enormous changes in the types of leisure pursuits that have taken place since Victorian times. The range of learning experiences and fun activities for children has greatly increased, to include a wide range of outdoor pursuits previously considered mainly the preserve of adults. Often organised by schools, day trips, camps and activites like this are useful and fun ways of learning, relaxing, exercising and interacting with schoolmates. This is in direct contrast to the strict, rigid, highly disciplined school lessons of the Victorian era and its disinterest in children's rights and needs.

These canoes are skilfully designed for comfort, ease of use and buoyancy. They are made from fibreglass, a material noted for its strength and lightness. Fibreglass is used in a wide range of products, including things that need to be lightweight for speed, such as motorbikes and other watercraft. In Victorian times, materials like this had not been developed. This picture provides a vivid contrast to the Victorian images of children playing or reading.

Skateboarding

Skateboarding is a popular modern pursuit that did not exist until the latter half of the 20th century. Fibreglass is often used in the manufacture of skateboards, surfboards and snowboards for lightness and speed. Skateboarding tends to be a leisure pursuit largely followed by boys and young men. It requires great agility, balance and strength and the boards can go at considerable speeds, but it can take place almost anywhere where there is concrete or tarmac. It is also a somewhat hazardous pastime and bones are sometimes broken as well as other injuries sustained. Specialist clothing is now commonly worn when skateboarding, such as wide, strong trainers for a good grip on the board, and helmets and knee and elbow pads to protect these parts of the body from grazing when the inevitable happens! There is a whole fashion style based around the skater look.

Boarding has featured in Hollywood movies and, like surfing, snowboarding and BMX-biking, has specialist tournaments and competitions dedicated to it. It has become glamorised as a rather 'macho' pursuit. Successful professional skaters like Tony Hawks can be very high earners and generate computer-game spin-offs among other merchandising opportunities.

Discussing the photographs

▶ Look at the images with the class and ask them what they show. Ask if anyone in the class has taken part in these kinds of activity.

▶ Talk about leisure pursuits in the past and compare them with modern activities. Consider how much leisure has changed, particularly for children, compared with the 19th century, and which of the activities discussed are new to the 20th or 21st centuries.

▶ Ask the children to tell you about the leisure activities they like to do. Which do they think would have been possible in Victorian times? Do they, for example, still enjoy reading, playing football, skipping, playing board games?

▶ Clarify that the first picture shows a canoeing lesson on a lake, while the second is of a skateboarder.

▶ Ask the children to name the equipment shown, for example oar, lifejacket, canoe, skateboard, elbow pads, helmet.

▶ Tell the children about the special material used to make the hulls of canoes, some skateboards and surfboards – fibreglass.

▶ Talk about other materials that have been created in modern times, like many plastics, fibre optics, Teflon and so on. Explain that these materials did not exist in Victorian times, and that they are by-products of the 20th and 21st centuries' petro-chemical industries and the space age.

Activities

▶ Ask any children who have experience of canoeing or skateboarding to describe what they have done. Get them to talk about the canoes they used, and the special feature of the canoes. Ask them if it was arranged by the school. Do the same with the children who have experience of skateboarding or surfing. Ask the rest of the class to make notes while listening.

▶ After research, create a class book or database about inventions, such as Teflon, that have been made during the space age and how these inventions came about.

▶ Organise the class into groups and allocate them one each of 'Playing marbles', 'Playing with a hoop', 'Sliding on the ice', 'Learning to cook', 'Pegging out washing' and 'Reading at home' (provided on the CD). Ask the children to list comparisons between that image and either 'Canoeing' or 'Skateboarding'. Encourage them to focus on how and where the activity would take place and the equipment needed. Help them to write a concluding summary on how much has changed, making reference to details in the pictures to justify their ideas.

▶ Set the children the task of writing an adventure story about a boy or girl on a canoeing holiday.

NOTES ON THE PHOTOCOPIABLE PAGES

Word cards PAGES 24–7

The word cards build on those suggested in the QCA units and introduce a number of specific types of vocabulary, including words related to:

▶ child labour, such as: factories, mines, inspector
▶ poor children, such as: orphanage, workhouse, destitute, plight
▶ legislation, such as: Act of Parliament, factory report, law, House of Lords
▶ education, such as: board schools, slates, inkwell

Encourage the children to think of other appropriate words to add to those provided, in order to build up a word bank for the theme of Victorian Britain. They could include words encountered in their researches, such as overlooker, textile, industry, philanthropist, in relation to discoveries about child labour in Victorian times. They could also use the cards in labelling displays and in writing simple and complex sentences to record what they have learned. They should also use the word cards as support in descriptive, factual and creative work and in making notes for discussions and arguments.

Activities

▶ Once you have made copies of the word cards, cut them out and laminate them. Use them as often as possible when talking about the Victorians and in word games

▶ Add further vocabulary to the set of words, using those suggested by the children.

▶ Add the words to a class word bank and encourage the children to use the words in stories and non-fiction writing as often as possible.

▶ Ask the children to create sentences of their own using the word cards, to summarise their learning about Victorian Britain.

▶ Devise wordsearches, crossword puzzles and Hangman games, using specific sets of words related to the current topic, such as words to do with the monarchy.

▶ Make cloze procedures, omitting key words from a text. Encourage the children to write the words without support.

Timeline of Victorian Britain

PAGE 28

This timeline can be used to introduce children to chronology over a specific, recognisable span of time. It includes significant dates in Victoria's life, as well as key events in British history and cultural and technological changes that affected society. It also refers to important legislation on work, education and health, which affected the lives of the poor in particular. The fairly short span of time contains a large number of significant events and the timeline helps to emphasise how rapid and fundamental the pace of change was in Victorian Britain, and how much the lives of people changed as a result of new technologies.

This timeline could be used alongside pictures from Victorian Britain to give children some visual representation of chronological sequence and of changes that took place. It could be adapted for the classroom in the form of a long string that could be stretched across the classroom. Alternatively, it could be adapted to create a large wall frieze to which the children could add other information about significant figures such as Lord Shaftesbury and Dr Barnardo.

The kind of timeline shown here can also be useful at the end of a topic, for checking children's success in grasping ideas of sequence, chronology, change and understanding of dates. This could be carried out by asking children to create their own version of a Victorian timeline, or by giving them a blank outline to complete by positioning key events in the correct order and pictures and labels in the appropriate places.

Discussing the timeline
▶ At the beginning of the topic, ask the children what they think this timeline shows.
▶ Clarify what the dates on the timeline mean. Explain that this line with captioned dates represents the passing of time.
▶ Talk about key events during the life of Queen Victoria and add more labels as appropriate.
▶ Point out the wars mentioned, and discuss how many wars have taken place in recent years, such as in the Gulf, the Falklands and the Balkans.
▶ Notice the large number of important inventions and technological advances achieved, and tell the children that the Victorian era was a period of rapid scientific growth.
▶ Use the timeline in discussions about causes and the effects of key legislation and economic developments.
▶ Use the fiction and non-fiction texts on the photocopiable pages and the pictures provided on the CD to illustrate the discussion about the timeline.

Activities
▶ Make a class timeline using this one as an example. Ask the children to put any other picture from the period they find or create themselves, in the appropriate places on the timeline.
▶ Give the children a blank timeline with either key dates or events; and ask them to add relevant pictures in the right places. More advanced children could create their own timeline, using their own preferred 'template'.

The carding-room

PAGE 29

This extract, although fictional, gives what is probably a fairly accurate account of one of the work-related illnesses that textile workers suffered from during the 19th century. What makes the extract particularly poignant is the knowledge that at least one means of reducing the risk of these often fatal illnesses (the extractor wheel) was well known, but because this would have cost money, it was not put into practice in the mill that Bessie worked in.

Discussing the extract
▶ Tell the children that this is an extract from a novel. Read the text to the children first, before reading it together, as the dialect can be easier to hear than read.
▶ Explain a few of the difficult words in dialect, like *nesh* which means 'timid' and *soft*, meaning 'weak'. Gradely meant respectable, or good-looking if used about a girl.
▶ Explain what went on in a carding-room and why such a lot of fluff was generated.
▶ Ask the children why this should make the workers ill.
▶ See if anyone can remember from the text what one solution was to this problem and discuss why this was not used in the mill Bessie worked in.
▶ What do the children think of Bessie's attitude to this? Should she and her family have tried to do something about it? What may have happened to them if they had spoken up?

▶ Ask the children what they think might happen to Bessie.
▶ Discuss working conditions in general at that time, for example in mines as well as mills.

Activities
See 'Mill rules', below.

Mill rules PAGE 30

These rules are taken from an original source used in a Victorian mill in Haslingden in Lancashire, and were fairly typical. They illustrate the harsh working conditions in force at that time. They also show how workers were penalised financially for any kind of problem that was encountered, despite these sometimes being beyond their control. Any financial penalty would have been serious for people on such low wages.

Discussing the text
▶ Read the rules through with the child, and ask them what kind of text this is. (A set of rules, instructions.)
▶ Discuss what the overlookers were. (Supervisors, who didn't do manual work themselves.)
▶ Consider whether all of these offences were necessarily caused by the workers, for example the bobbins breaking. Talk about the fairness of these rules and how restrictive and unreasonable they seem to be.
▶ Compare these rules with, for example, your school rules and the motives behind them. Do the mill rules emphasise safety for the employees?
▶ Discuss the significance of fines imposed on very poor people.
▶ Explain 'old money' to the children, and the meaning of 2d as 2p, the d coming from the Latin word *denarius*, an old name for a penny.

Activities
▶ Challenge the children to research another Victorian industry, for example pottery, and write a list of rules for those workers. Tell them to think about how these rules would have different functions and requirements but would probably be just as strict.
▶ Working with the whole class, devise some rules for a modern-day factory in Britain, taking into account modern working conditions and the rights of the workers.
▶ If possible, take the class to visit a working mill. In school, allow time for groups to enact short dramas on some of the work in the mill. Encourage the children to develop their dramas to include characters such as Bessie from 'The carding-room' on photocopiable page 29.
▶ The children could write short stories based on a day in the life of a child working in this mill. Encourage them to include the child's feelings of tiredness, fear, ill-health, and the oppressive, miserable working atmosphere.

Biography of Lord Shaftesbury PAGE 31

The brief outlines of the lives and work of Lord Shaftesbury and Dr Barnardo provide some factual information that can be used as a starting point for further work. Shaftesbury was an important figure in Victorian Britain and, after something of a slow start in his political career, achieved some considerable successes on behalf of children. This text is intended to show the indefatigable nature of the work he pursued, in the face of great opposition, and how he returned to issues when he knew that legislation was not being enforced or did not go far enough. It might be of interest to compare the living and working conditions of Victorian children with those of many children in the developing countries today.

Discussing the text
▶ Ask the children what kind of text this is. (A biography.)
▶ Discuss the kind of background that Shaftesbury came from. What kind of school did he attend? What kind of education did he receive? Compare this with the lack of education for the children of poor families in the early 19th century.
▶ Ask the children why they think he began to be interested in the plight of poor children.
▶ Consider steps he could take to do something about the situation with which he disagreed.
▶ Ask the children why the new laws were not always carried out. (The greed and pride of the bosses, the lack of inspectors.)

▶ Ask the children what they think it would be like if they did not have to come to school! Discuss how there might be short-term advantages, but also considerable disadvantages. Talk about all the things they would not be able to do when they were older.

Activities
See 'Biography of Dr Barnardo' below, for activities on both texts.

Biography of Dr Barnardo
PAGE 32

Barnardo's family and social background was quite different from that of Shaftesbury (although they were hardly at opposite ends of the social scale), and it is interesting to see how the paths of the two men crossed and they collaborated in some of their work.

Discussing the text
▶ Ask the children what Barnardo originally intended to do. (Missionary work.) Consider what this indicates to us about the kind of person he was.
▶ Talk about how he noticed the poor children and was appalled by the kind of lives they had.
▶ Ask the children why he had such strong feelings about people drinking alcohol, and what he did about this.
▶ Discuss how he raised money and how he set up homes for orphans.
▶ Ask the children to imagine what it must have been like for children sent away to Australia or Canada. Explain that many of these people have since returned to find their relatives.

Activities
▶ Ask the children to add the dates of the two men's lives to the timeline on photocopiable page 28.
▶ Ask groups of children to find out different information about Lord Shaftesbury and Dr Barnardo, using books, packs and the Internet. Combine the details to construct longer biographies.
▶ Take on the role of either Shaftesbury or Barnardo and let the children ask questions about what you decided to do.
▶ *The Big Ship Sails* from Scholastic's *Performance Plays* series includes a moving and informative playscript that you might help the children to perform.
▶ Help the children to find out about the way bills were proposed and passed in government and how they also had to be approved by the House of Lords, as they do now.

Dotheboys Hall
PAGE 33

This text, together with the 'School inspector's report' (photocopiable page 34) provides a useful resource for learning about school life in Victorian times. This extract from a Dickens novel gives an indication of what passed for education in many early schools, and although dealt with in a light-hearted way, carries a serious message about the quality of the education that children were receiving, even in fee-paying schools.

Dickens knew what it was like to suffer from poverty, as when he was a child his father was sent to Marshalsea debtor's prison for several months, and Charles had to work sealing and labelling bottles of shoe-blacking. It was possibly as a consequence of having lived through hardships himself that Dickens held strong views on social reform and worked hard to draw attention to the suffering of the poor, particularly children.

Discussing the extract
▶ Explain to the children who Charles Dickens was and give them a bit of background to the views he held.
▶ Explain any difficult vocabulary and sentence structure to help the children appreciate the extract fully. It may be best for you to read it to them first.
▶ Allow the children to enjoy the humour in the extract, but draw out the serious issue of poor education behind it.
▶ Discuss what kind of education the children in this school are receiving.
▶ Ask the children what they think the children are mainly engaged in doing.
▶ Do they think this is a good school? Is the master is a good teacher?
▶ Ask them if this is a school they would like to attend.

Activities
See 'School inspector's report', below.

School inspector's report
PAGE 34

This report extract, adapted from an original source, shows not only the style of teaching and learning that took place in Victorian times, but also the attitudes of teachers and inspectors towards it. 'Learning' seemed to consist entirely of memorisation and repetition. Writing, in this case, is copywriting, involving no original thought or creativity on the part of the children, who were seen only as passive recipients of existing wisdom.

Discussing the text
▶ Discuss what kind of text this is. Ask the children who wrote it and why.
▶ Establish what subject the inspector was looking at. (Some form of RE.) Explain that the Catechism is a form of religious instruction as a set of questions and answers.
▶ Consider what the text tells us about schools in Victorian Britain.
▶ Ask the children if they would have liked to have been pupils in this school.

Activities
▶ Ask the children to compare the two texts and summarise what each one tells us about schools in Victorian Britain.
▶ Ask the children to carry out some research of their own into Victorian schools. Suggest they find out about the different kinds of schools that existed.
▶ Compare this School Inspector's report with a modern day summary from an Ofsted report.
▶ Ask the children to compare the inspector's report with the images 'Typewriting lesson' and 'Playing marbles'. Let them discuss the things they would have liked and disliked, and then to write a short account of a day in the life of a Victorian school child, either a boy or girl.

Jubilee celebration
PAGE 35

This fiction extract gives children an insight into some of the leisure pursuits of ordinary working people in Victorian times. Set at the time of Victoria's Golden Jubilee, it describes many of the simple games and entertainments that were organised as part of a village fête to celebrate the occasion. Children will recognise many of these, but some will probably be strange to them, such as climbing the greased pole. The story also gives a good insight into the social divisions that were so significant in Victorian times. Flora Thompson's clever use of language highlights the contrast in appearance and behaviour between the classes and the relief felt when the local gentry leave.

Discussing the text
▶ Ask the children what is happening in the story.
▶ Find volunteers to list the types of entertainments mentioned that they recognise.
▶ Discuss the 'greased pole' game, and ask if anyone has ever seen this done.
▶ Talk about what eventually happened in this competition, and whether it was fair. Does a leg of mutton seem like a great prize to us today?
▶ Ask a volunteer to describe how the villagers felt in the presence of the local *gentlepeople* (gentry). Consider why this spoiled their fun and how they felt when the gentry moved on.

Activities
▶ Compare these celebrations with a modern event of a similar kind, such as a town carnival or school fête, and ask the children to write a brief comparison, noting what has stayed the same and what has changed. The recent Golden Jubilee celebrations for Elizabeth II would make an interesting comparison.
▶ Provide art materials and ask the children to create their own artistic impression of this Victorian day out.
▶ Divide the class into groups of villagers and some gentry, and ask them to create scenes from the fête. Help the groups to write brief playscripts and then provide time for performances.
▶ Ask the children to make a series of illustrations about Victorian pastimes and leisure, such as the activities mentioned in this text and others on the CD, such as 'Sliding on the ice'. Collect these into a class book.

factories

mines

mills

rules

supervisor

inspector

machinery

conditions

Child poverty word cards

orphan
orphanage
workhouse
homeless
destitute
plight
slum
care home

Act of Parliament
factory report
mine report
law
politician
House of Lords
Bill
reform

Victorian education word cards

board schools

monitors

logbooks

slates

inkwell

inspection

Timeline of Victorian Britain

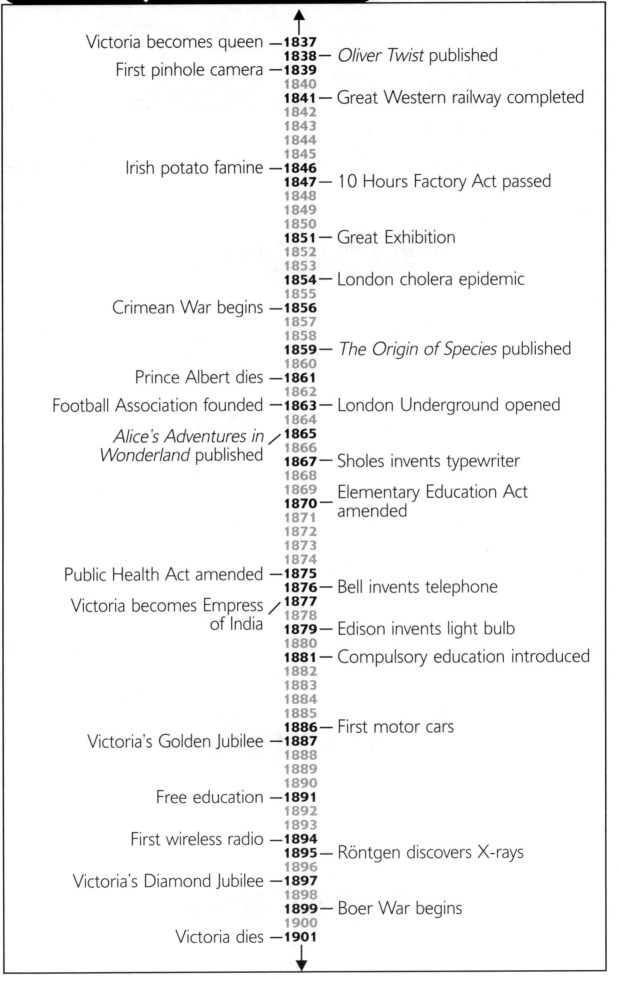

Victoria becomes queen — **1837**	
1838 —	*Oliver Twist* published
First pinhole camera — **1839**	
1840	
1841 —	Great Western railway completed
1842	
1843	
1844	
1845	
Irish potato famine — **1846**	
1847 —	10 Hours Factory Act passed
1848	
1849	
1850	
1851 —	Great Exhibition
1852	
1853	
1854 —	London cholera epidemic
1855	
Crimean War begins — **1856**	
1857	
1858	
1859 —	*The Origin of Species* published
1860	
Prince Albert dies — **1861**	
1862	
Football Association founded — **1863** —	London Underground opened
1864	
Alice's Adventures in ╱ **1865**	
Wonderland published	1866
1867 —	Sholes invents typewriter
1868	
1869	Elementary Education Act
1870 —	amended
1871	
1872	
1873	
1874	
Public Health Act amended — **1875**	
1876 —	Bell invents telephone
Victoria becomes Empress ╱ **1877**	
of India	1878
1879 —	Edison invents light bulb
1880	
1881 —	Compulsory education introduced
1882	
1883	
1884	
1885	
1886 —	First motor cars
Victoria's Golden Jubilee — **1887**	
1888	
1889	
1890	
Free education — **1891**	
1892	
1893	
First wireless radio — **1894**	
1895 —	Röntgen discovers X-rays
1896	
Victoria's Diamond Jubilee — **1897**	
1898	
1899 —	Boer War begins
1900	
Victoria dies — **1901**	

The carding-room

"I think I was well when mother died, but I have never been rightly strong sin' somewhere about that time. I began to work in a carding-room soon after, and the fluff got into my lungs, and poisoned me."

"Fluff?" said Margaret, inquiringly.

"Fluff," repeated Bessie. "Little bits, as fly off fro' the cotton, when they're carding it, and fill the air till it looks all fine white dust. They say it winds round the lungs, and tightens them up. Anyhow, there's many a one as works in a carding-room, that falls into a waste, coughing and spitting blood, because they're just poisoned by the fluff."

"But can't it be helped?" asked Margaret.

"I dunno. Some folk have a great wheel at one end o' their carding-rooms to make a draught, and carry off th' dust; but that wheel costs a deal o' money – five or six hundred pound, maybe, and brings in no profit; so it's but a few of th' masters as will put 'em up; and I've heard tell o' men who didn't like working in places where there was a wheel, because they said as how it made 'em hungry, at after they'd been long used to swallowing fluff, to go without it, and that their wage ought to be raised if they were to work in such places. So between masters and men th' wheels fall through. I know I wish there'd been a wheel in our place, though."

"Did not your father know about it?" asked Margaret.

"Yes! And he were sorry. But our factory were a good one on the whole; and a steady likely set o' people; and father was afeard of letting me go to a strange place, for though yo' would na think it now, many a one then used to call me a gradely less enough. And I did na like to be reckoned nesh and soft, and Mary's schooling were to be kept up, mother said, and father he were always liking to buy books, and go to lectures o' one kind or another – all which took money – so I just worked on till I shall ne'er get the whirr out o' my ears, or the fluff out o' my throad i' this world. That's all."

from *North and South* by Elizabeth Gaskell

Rules

to be Observed by the Hands Employed in This Mill.

Rule 1.   All the Overlookers shall be on the premises first and last.

Rule 2.   Any person coming too late shall be fined as follows:– for 5 minutes 2d, 10 minutes 4d, and 15 minutes 6d, etc.

Rule 3.   For any bobbins found on the floor 1d for each bobbin.

Rule 4.   For any loose ends 2d for each single end.

Rule 5.   For waste on the floor 2d.

Rule 6.   For any oil wasted or spilled on the floor 2d each offence, besides paying for the value of the oil.

Rule 7.   For any broken bobbins, they shall be paid for according to their value.

Rule 8.   Any person leaving their work and found talking with any of the other work people shall be fined 2d for each offence.

Rule 9.   For any oath or insolent language, 3d for the first offence, and if repeated they shall be dismissed.

Rule 10.   The machinery shall be swept and cleaned down every meal time.

The Overlookers are strictly enjoined to attend to these Rules, and they will be responsible to the Masters for the Workpeople observing them.

Water-foot Mill, Near Haslingden, September, 1851.

■ SCHOLASTIC
PHOTOCOPIABLE

Biography of Lord Shaftesbury

Anthony Ashley Cooper was born in 1801. He was given the title Lord Ashley from the age of 10 and became the Earl of Shaftesbury in 1851. He went to boarding school when he was 7 and later studied at Oxford University. At the age of 25, he became a Member of Parliament. In his new role, he began to take an interest in the plight of poor children after reading newspaper reports about child labour in industry.

In 1833, Lord Ashley proposed that children should work for a maximum of 10 hours a day but this bill was defeated in Parliament. However, the government accepted that children needed protecting and decided to put forward its own proposals, and later in the year the Factory Act was passed.

It was now illegal for children under 9 to be employed in textile factories, and children between 9 and 13 must not work for more than 8 hours a day. A disappointment for the reformers, however, was that children over 13 were still allowed to work for up to 12 hours a day. The campaigners were also concerned that only 4 inspectors were available to ensure the law was carried out. They maintained that factory owners would continue to exploit young children.

In 1842, Lord Ashley had the Coal Mines Act approved by Parliament and, as a result, women and children were not allowed to work underground. He also continued his work for improved working hours for children in factories. He published a report in 1863 stating that some factories still had children of 4 and 5 working from 6 in the morning until 10 at night.

Another social interest for Lord Shaftesbury was education for working class children. He was chairman of the Ragged Schools Union, an organisation that had set up over a hundred schools for poor children by 1850. Lord Shaftesbury died in 1885.

Biography of Dr Barnardo

Born in Dublin in 1845, Thomas Barnardo first worked as an office clerk. During this time, he became involved with evangelism. He then moved to London where he studied medicine. He planned to travel to China as a missionary, but when he became aware of the plight of the poor and homeless children of London itself, he turned his attention to this issue.

He opened a Ragged School in Stepney, and began raising money to set up homes for these street children. Support was given by Lord Shaftesbury and the banker Robert Barclay, and Barnardo was able to establish his first home for destitute and orphaned children in 1868. The children would be well fed, looked after and educated while in his care.

A committed Christian, Dr Barnardo was deeply concerned by the enormous quantities of alcohol that many people drank in those days. He saw this as a major reason for illness and poverty. He would protest and set up mission tents on behalf of the Temperance Society outside public houses. In 1872, he bought a well-known 'gin palace' in London and converted it into a church, which contained Britain's first coffee house.

Meanwhile, Barnardo continued working for his children's homes. He began to photograph the boys in the Stepney Home just as they arrived (sometimes contriving to make them appear in worse condition than they may actually have been) and then again a few months later when they had recovered from their experiences of life on the streets. He sold these pictures in small packs, raising funds and increasing the profile of his charitable work.

Ten years after opening his first children's home, Dr Barnardo was running 50 orphanages in London. He also established the Village Home for Girls in Ilford, which housed over 1000 children, and set up 'boarding out' schemes.

One of Dr Barnado's last, and more controversial, enterprises was a scheme for sending children to Australia and Canada, in the hope of providing them with a better life. By the time he died in 1905, he had sent over 18 000 children to start new lives in Australia and Canada.

■ SCHOLASTIC
PHOTOCOPIABLE

Dotheboys Hall

This extract tells of Nicholas Nickleby's first day as assistant to Mr Wackford Squeers at his Academy, Dotheboys Hall.

They ranged themselves in front of the schoolmaster's desk – half-a-dozen scarecrows, out at knees and elbows, one of whom placed a torn and filthy book beneath his learned eye.

"This is the first class in English spelling and philosophy, Nickleby," said Squeers, beckoning Nicholas to stand beside him… "Now, where's the first boy?"

"Please, sir, he's cleaning the back-parlour window," said the temporary head of the philosophical class.

"So he is, to be sure," rejoined Squeers. "We go upon the practical mode of teaching, Nickleby; the regular education system. C-l-e-a-n, clean, verb active, to make bright, to scour. W-i-n, win, d-e-r, der, winder, a casement. When the boy knows this out of the book, he goes and does it. It's just the same principle as the use of the globes. Where's the second boy?"

"Please, sir, he's weeding the garden," replied a small voice.

"To be sure," said Squeers, by no means disconcerted. "So he is. B-o-t, bot, t-i-n, tin, n-e-y, ney, bottinney, noun substantive, a knowledge of plants. When he has learned that bottinney means a knowledge of plants, he goes and knows 'em. That's our system, Nickleby: what do you think of it?"

"It's a very useful one, at any rate," answered Nicholas.

"I believe you," rejoined Squeers… "Third boy, what's a horse?"

"A beast, sir," replied the boy.

"So it is," said Squeers. "Ain't it, Nickleby?"

"I believe there is no doubt of that, sir," answered Nicholas.

"Of course there isn't," said Squeers. "A horse is a quadruped, and quadruped's Latin for beast, as everybody that's gone through the grammar knows, or else what's the use of having grammars at all?"

"Where, indeed!" said Nicholas abstractedly.

"As you're perfect in that," resumed Squeers, turning to the boy, "go and look after *my* horse, and rub him down well, or I'll rub you down. The rest of the class go and draw water up, till somebody tells you to leave off, for it's washing-day tomorrow, and they want the coppers filled."

from *Nicholas Nickleby* by Charles Dickens

Report of School Inspection

School: St. James, Cruikshaw.   Mixed.

Local Authority: Lancashire.   *Parish:* St James, Cruikshaw

Date of Inspection: July 10th, 1897.   *Inspector:* The Rev. T. Smith.

REPORT

The method of the opening of the School is satisfactory for the Training of the children in Religious Instruction, and the hymn singing and repetition of the Lord's Prayer are good.

The Teaching of both the Old and New Testament is good throughout the School, and the children have learned their lessons well, being able to repeat the Instructed parts without fault. The younger children, however, will need to be more strictly Instructed in their diligence in committing the necessary lines to memory.

The Repetition and Catechism are well known, but more attention should be paid to clear enunciation. Some female pupils, especially, did not speak out with the desired clarity.

On the whole the standard of written work is good, with the children developing a very good hand in their copywriting.

Remarks

A further copy of the Old and New Testaments would be helpful to the masters.

■SCHOLASTIC
PHOTOCOPIABLE

Jubilee celebration

This fiction extract is about the activities that took place in a small rural village on the day of Queen Victoria's Golden Jubilee. The villagers have just had tea in the park, in a huge marquee, and there are a roundabout, hurdy-gurdy and coconut shies among other entertainments.

After tea there were sports, with races, high jumps, dipping heads into tubs of water to retrieve sixpences with the teeth, grinning through horse-collars, the prize going to the one making the most grotesque face, and, to crown all, climbing the greased pole for the prize leg of mutton. This was a tough job, as the pole was as tall and slender as a telephone post and extremely slippery. Prudent wives would not allow their husbands to attempt it on account of spoiling their clothes, so the competition was left to the ragamuffins and a few experts who had had the foresight to bring with them a pair of old trousers. This competition must have run concurrently with the other events, for all the afternoon there was a crowd around it, and first one, then another, would 'have a go'. It was painful to watch the climbers, shinning up a few inches, then slipping back again, and, as one retired, another taking his place, until, late in the afternoon, the champion arrived, climbed slowly but steadily to the top and threw down the joint, which, by the way, must have been already roasted after four or five hours in the burning sun. It was whispered around that he had carried a bag of ashes and sprinkled them on the greasy surface as he ascended.

The local gentlepeople promenaded the ground in parties: stout, red-faced squires, raising their straw hats to mop their foreheads; hunting ladies, incongruously garbed in silks and ostrich-feather boas; young girls in embroidered white muslin and boys in Eton suits. They had kind words for everybody, especially for the poor and lonely, and, from time to time, they would pause before some sight and try to enter into the spirit of the other beholders; but everywhere their arrival hushed the mirth, and there was a sigh of relief when they moved on. After dancing the first dance they disappeared, and 'now we can have some fun', the people said.

from *Lark Rise* by Flora Thompson

Photograph © Illustrated London News

VICTORIAN LOCAL HISTORY

Content, skills and concepts

This chapter relates to unit 12 of the QCA Scheme of Work and will assist in planning and resourcing work on the Victorian locality. It is assumed that this unit will be taught mainly to Year 5 or 6, and that it may also be adapted for earlier age groups. It suggests ways of investigating change within the Victorian period in the locality and the reasons for those changes. Children use their local area to explore characteristic features of life in the Victorian age and develop their sense of chronology, asking and answering questions from a range of sources.

Together with the Victorian Local History Resource Gallery on the CD-ROM, this chapter introduces a range of sources, including contemporary photographs, engravings and photographs taken in the present day. The chapter also provides materials to support the teaching of key historical concepts relevant to this period and theme.

Children will already have gained experience of using time-related vocabulary, asking and answering questions, and using visual and written sources. Recounting stories about the past, and looking for similarities and differences between the past and the present are prior learning activities that will have introduced relevant skills and concepts to the children before they progress to the skills and concepts in this unit. The chapter includes suggestions for the extension of these and other skills, such as recognising change and continuity and the ability to select and use information to support a discussion, for example about the reasons for changes in a local area.

Resources on the CD-ROM

Photographs and illustrations of transport forms, buildings and built environments are provided on the CD-ROM. Background information about these sources is provided in the teacher's notes, along with ideas for further work on them.

Photocopiable pages

Photocopiable resources at the end of the chapter (and also in PDF format on the CD) include:
- ▶ word and sentence cards that highlight the essential vocabulary of this topic
- ▶ guidelines for research
- ▶ a survey sheet listing features of Victorian buildings.

The teacher's notes that accompany the photocopiable pages include suggestions for developing discussion and for using the pages for whole class, group or individual activities. Some topic-specific vocabulary is included within the photocopiable texts. More able readers will be able to read and use these texts independently, but some children will need help in interpreting them.

History skills

Skills such as observation, description, the use of time-related vocabulary, sequencing, using a timeline, understanding the meaning of dates, comparing, inferring, listening, speaking, reading, writing and drawing are all involved in the activities suggested. For example, children can learn to use descriptive vocabulary to discuss the images provided on the CD.

Historical understanding

In the course of the suggested activities, a further aim is for children to develop more detailed knowledge of the past and their ability to sequence and date events independently, through their understanding of the context and content of the factual information they use. They will begin to give reasons for events and use primary sources to find further information. They will also have the opportunity to extend their skills in using descriptive language and specific time-related terms in writing their own factual accounts of the past. Communication skills of various types can be practised and developed in the course of this unit.

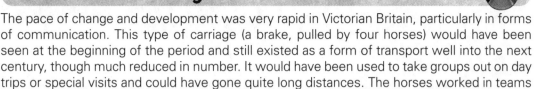

NOTES ON THE CD-ROM RESOURCES

Horse-drawn carriage

The pace of change and development was very rapid in Victorian Britain, particularly in forms of communication. This type of carriage (a brake, pulled by four horses) would have been seen at the beginning of the period and still existed as a form of transport well into the next century, though much reduced in number. It would have been used to take groups out on day trips or special visits and could have gone quite long distances. The horses worked in teams to pull such large, crowded vehicles.

Other forms of transport developed during Victoria's reign, so that the horse-drawn carriage was not the only kind of land transport available. There grew to be a variety of options by the end of the century, dominated by the railways. By the late Victorian period, most of these carriages were obsolete, and there are descriptions of them left lying around the countryside, rotting away or turned into hen coops.

Discussing the photograph
▶ Look at the picture and ask the children what they think is happening.
▶ Speculate where the carriage might be going or why it has brought these people here.
▶ Look at the detail on the carriage, for example the lantern, the cart wheels (large at the back and smaller at the front), the special seat for the drivers, high up at the front.
▶ Ask the children to describe what sort of journey passengers would have had in a carriage like this. Point out the fact that the wheels are solid, and ask the children to imagine what it would have been like going over a bumpy road.
▶ Think about the context of the photograph. Look particularly at the buildings and the layout of the street and discuss what may have changed and what has probably not. For example, many buildings like these are still to be seen, but the carriage and horses are not.

Activities
▶ Provide books, pamphlets, photographs and other pictures of your local area in Victorian times and ask the children to note the dates of each of their sources where possible. Ask them to note evidence of the type of transport used, then draw up a table in chronological order to show the different types of transport in use at different times within the period.
▶ Ask the children to comment on any trends that appear from these observations and then to write a short summary of the changes they have found.
▶ Suggest the children make a chronological sequence of pictures from their local area, showing forms of transport where possible.
▶ Challenge them to write an imaginative piece, describing a journey home in bad weather in a carriage like this one, after a long day out.

Steam train

In 1781, James Watt, a scientific instrument maker from Glasgow, had joined forces with Matthew Boulton, a Birmingham manufacturer, to create a steam engine that could turn wheels. This improvement to the steam engine was the technological development that most perhaps radically affected life in Victorian times. It was used in many different ways: to power looms and all kinds of factory and mining machinery, to power ships and trains and to operate agricultural machinery.

The steam train greatly affected the lives of most of the population. By 1879, trains could travel at over 96 kilometres an hour and travel became easy and cheap enough to be within the reach of most people. This meant that people could travel further to find work and for holidays and entertainment. Evidence of this change can be seen in the census records, if a comparison is made between those from 1851 and those from 1891 or 1901.

Discussing the photograph
▶ Discuss what kind of train is shown in this photograph.
▶ Ask the children if they think it is a train from the beginning or near the end of the Victorian age. Why? (Consider how fast the train seems to be going, the number of carriages it is pulling, the amount of track laid and the bridges built over the line.)

▶ Tell the children how early trains looked very different, with a tall funnel and a few open carriages, and they travelled at only 25 to 30 kilometres an hour. Nevertheless, at the time they were considered very dangerous because of their high speed.

▶ Look at the amount of steam and smoke being created by this more modern train. Ask the children why this was. If necessary, explain how the steam engine worked, powered by the burning of coal to heat steam, which then turned the wheels. Explain how this then resulted in both smoke and steam being produced.

▶ Ask if anyone has ever been for a journey on a steam train, and get them to describe their experience.

Activities

▶ Provide a wide range of resources from which the children can select pictures of steam trains as they developed. Suggest they try to find pictures from different dates within the Victorian period.

▶ Find where the railway lines run on a map of your locality. Get the children to locate the stations and investigate when the railways arrived in the local area. Are there fewer stations now than there used to be?

▶ Talk about the effects of rail travel on the local area. If possible, compare maps from early and late Victorian times to find where the railway tracks were laid and what had been there before.

▶ Discuss who was likely to have benefited from the arrival of the railways and look at the map to see who may have lost out, for example local farmers, whose land may have been built on.

▶ Give the children different roles and organise a Victorian class debate about whether the railway should be built in your area or not.

Railway station

Just 40 years after the opening of the first public railway in 1826, Victorian engineers created a massive railway network throughout the country, connecting towns, cities and ports. The whole enterprise was undertaken in great haste with companies in competition with each other, so that by the 1850s and 1860s, there were building works throughout the country, everywhere cluttered with heaps of masonry and half-finished structures. Other engineering projects also had to be constructed, such as tunnels, bridges, viaducts, cuttings and embankments. Railway stations were built in every locality and this often led to further buildings being constructed around the station. When completed, however, these stations were very impressive, innovative structures.

This illustration shows Birmingham Grand Central Station, which was built in 1854. This elegant, grand structure has a huge class roof built in a single span (the largest in the world at the time). It was a design common to many large stations and was also used in the Crystal Palace, created for the Great Exhibition of 1851. The design aimed partly to allow the trains to pass through unimpeded, but also to draw up smoke and steam away from the passengers on the platforms and make a light, airy building . Many cities were proud of their impressive stations, such as St Pancras in London, which was combined with a hotel. Elaborate wrought ironwork and carved wood was used extensively to enhance the grandeur of these buildings. Indeed, efficient transport was seen as a priority and matter of pride and no expense was spared to achieve it.

Discussing the picture

▶ Ask for volunteers to point out the key characteristics of the station, such as its great size, the high platforms, the bridges for the passengers and the huge high roof. Notice the bright sections of the platforms are from the sun coming through the roof.

▶ Ask the children to imagine what the passengers must have felt when they first used these brand new stations.

▶ Consider the number of railway lines going through the station, and talk about why there were so many.

▶ How did the passengers move around the station? How did they get from one platform to another?

▶ Discuss how the passengers knew when they could expect their train. Note the large clock, for example, and tell the children that timetables were soon drawn up for all the trains so that people knew when to go to the station to catch them. Explain that the Victorians were proud that their trains ran on time.

▶ Help the children to imagine the various sights, sounds and smells of a railway station like this and describe them.

Activities

▶ Look at a map of Britain and consider the huge railway network that was created in only about 40 years. Look on the map for the stations in your locality.

▶ If possible, arrange a visit to a local station that was built in Victorian times. Before the visit, ensure that the children are familiar with the characteristic features of Victorian buildings, by referring to 'Features of Victorian buildings' on photocopiable page 51 and ask them to note these during their visit. They can also make sketches of the details.

▶ Compare the number of lines, the bridges and so on in the Birmingham station with busy stations today, like New Street itself (the replacement for Grand Central) and London Euston.

▶ Let the children carry out some of their own research to find out who were the great railway engineers and architects of the Victorian stations, for example Isambard Kingdom Brunel and Gilbert Scott (the designer of St Pancras Station in London). They can try to discover who built their local railway and explore what other work he carried out in the local area.

▶ Get the children to work in pairs to list the changes that the building of the railway station would have brought about in the locality. Stress that there were negative changes (for example reduced business for canals and coaching inns, damage to landscape) as well as positive (reduced journey times, greater availability of goods and leisure). At the end of the session, the children can compare notes.

Paddle steamer

The paddle steamer shown in this photograph, the *Adder*, was powered by a steam engine, and it was the development of steamships that revolutionised sea travel during the Victorian age. Not reliant on the winds and weather, steam-powered ships could travel at greater speeds and were more reliable than sailing ships. In the 19th century, as steamship design developed, steel began to be used rather than iron. Steel is stronger and lighter and allowed the ships to travel faster. Isambard Kingdom Brunel was one of the pioneers of steam transport (among other communication engineering), building the SS *Great Eastern*, which was the largest passenger ship of its time and could carry 4000 passengers. The *Adder*, shown here, was built to sail from Greenock on the west of Scotland to Belfast as part of a daily mail service. She was a fast steamer and also carried passengers who would take day trips. Many paddle steamers were sea-going vessels.

Discussing the picture

▶ Ask the children what kind of ship is shown in this photograph.

▶ Discuss the smoke and steam emerging from it and discuss the reasons for this. If necessary, explain the working of the steam engine in powering the ship.

▶ Discuss why the ships were called *steamers*. Note the paddle at each side of the steamer and explain how this propelled the ship forward.

▶ Talk about how iron ships were common at the beginning of the 19th century and how steel gradually began to be used instead. Ask the children if they can think of any reasons for this change. (Steel was lighter and stronger.)

▶ Ask if anyone has ever travelled on a paddle steamer and encourage them to relate their experience to the class.

Activities

▶ On a map of Britain, identify the major ports. Look at a map of the locality and find the nearest port. Discuss the kind of port it is and whether ships have sailed from it. Consider whether the ships might have carried passengers or freight.

▶ Suggest that children use the school library and the Internet to search for information about famous Victorian steamers, such as the *Great Eastern*.

▶ Ask the children to work in pairs to write brief biographies of Victorian engineers, such as Isambard Kingdom Brunel.

▶ If possible, organise a visit such as to see and walk around the SS *Great Britain*, one of Brunel's ships, in Bristol.

Ocean liner being built

Shipbuilding was for many years, right into the 20th century, a major industry in Britain. Tyneside, Barrow, Belfast, Glasgow and Birkenhead were important shipbuilding centres, particularly because they had access to local coal, iron and steel works. Shipbuilding on a large scale affected these localities significantly and most of the local male population would have been involved in the industry in some way. The building of large ocean-going passenger liners and freight carriers also affected virtually every locality in the British Isles, in the sense that worldwide travel became more accessible and the availability of imported produce increased. There was also a lot of labour migration to shipbuilding areas. There was a wider variety of goods from abroad and they became cheaper as a result of the capacity of these large ships to transport goods more widely. The increasing speed of these ships meant that new produce, such as tropical fruit, became available in Britain on a large scale for the first time.

Discussing the picture

▶ Ask the children to study this illustration carefully, and to tell you what they think it shows. Explain that this is a large ocean-going ship being built in a shipyard.

▶ Ask volunteers to point out the features of the ship that are most striking to them, for example its great size.

▶ See if the children can work out how many decks the ship will have (Possibly four or five.)

▶ Discuss whether it is going to be a passenger ship or a freight ship. Point out that there appear to be portholes along the sides where the decks will be, suggesting that it is to be for passengers.

▶ Look at the way the ship is being made and point out that it is constructed in sections that are being welded and bolted together.

▶ Point out the number of people that can be seen working on the ship and talk about the impact of an industry such as this on the local community, for example in employing most of the working men in the area.

▶ Ask how a shipyard worker might have felt when a new ship he had helped to build was launched.

Activities

▶ On a map of Britain, find the places where the major shipyards mentioned above used to be. Ask the children to carry out their own investigations into the shipyards and the type of ships that were built there. Make a large wall map and illustrate it with pictures of the ships that were made.

▶ Discuss the impact on your local area of new produce that was brought to Britain. Use information from the trade directories for the locality to judge the impact of this new produce on the local shops. Trade directories are available in libraries and record offices, and show what kind of shops were present and their occupants and owners. Ask the children to write a brief account of any changes that took place in the local area during Victorian times and speculate whether the changes may have been a result of better transport and communications.

▶ Consider the opportunities for wider travel and for immigration and emigration on these large ships. Get the children to look at the census data for their locality to see if people began to arrive from other parts of the world during the Victorian period. There was a great deal of immigration, particularly from Ireland, into some parts of the country, especially into certain areas in the large towns and cities, such as Manchester.

Colliery

This is a contemporary oil painting by W. Wheldon, showing a colliery in the Northumberland and Durham coalfield in about 1845. The painting shows the pithead and kilns. As can be seen, the colliery was a very large, elaborate structure, which incorporated buildings, large pulleys, chimneys, kilns and small railways. The winding gear for raising and lowering workers and coal was housed in its own large building. Here there would also be a huge steam engine that powered the winding gear.

The colliery would be an important part of the local community, as it would have employed a significant number of the local population, including children, who would often have to work to supplement their parents' wages for the family to earn enough to live on. The pithead would be a prominent feature, and would have dominated the skyline in some localities.

Discussing the painting

▶ Ask the children what this painting shows, and explain that it is called the pithead, the part of a coal mine that can be seen above the ground. Discuss how the mechanical structures at the pithead would be a prominent feature of the landscape of a mining town or village.

▶ Look at each part of the pithead and discuss its function. For example, the winding gear lifted and lowered cages of coal, equipment and miners up and down in the shaft leading down to the coalface. Point out that this lifting gear was very large and would have been worked by a steam engine. This is why there is a chimney stack giving out smoke – from the burning coal used to heat water to produce steam.

▶ Look at the tracks in the foreground of the picture, and discuss what these were for. Note the steam engine and truck loaded with coal.

▶ Notice the details that tell us how long ago the painting was set, for example the ponies and carts, the people's dress, as well as the old-fashioned mining equipment.

▶ Focus on the big heaps just visible on the right of the picture, and explain that these were heaps of waste material extracted as part of the mining process. Sometimes they were known as 'slag' heaps, and grew to great heights in coal mining areas. Consider the effect of these, and the colliery buildings, on the local community. Mention some of the dangers of slag heaps, such as the disaster at Aberfan in 1966.

▶ Discuss how widespread mining was and its importance in the industrialisation of the country. Talk about how the closure of a colliery could be a disaster for a local community, as lots of people's work depended upon it. Many collieries closed during the 20th century.

Activities

▶ Provide further information and images of the work of children in mines during the first part of the 19th century (see 'Child labour in a mine' and 'Inside a mine' in the Victorian Britain Resource Gallery). Help the children to make a wall display, adding their own captions.

▶ If possible, visit the site of an old mine, to learn about conditions at first hand.

▶ Provide information about the working of mines in the 19th century, for the children to research the equipment used and the jobs that were done.

▶ Give each child an outline map of Britain and work with the whole class to mark on it the places where large amounts of coal were mined. The children could also find out where slate and tin mining took place and devise a key to show these different industries on their map. Ask the children to make brief notes about the effects of the mines on their local area.

Textile mill

The more effective use of steam as a source of power transformed industry at the end of the 18th century and into the 19th and had a dramatic effect on the physical and social geography of the country. Industries such as iron and textile production developed where coal was easily available. Thousands of textile mills were built in the Midlands and North of England and the iron industry expanded in Wales, Scotland and the Midlands. Towns grew where there was industry and many rural areas transformed into industrial centres. People moved to where there was work, many moving from the country to live and work in the towns. This illustration is of the United Mill in Werneth, Oldham.

Many people grew very wealthy as a consequence of industrialisation, for example mill and factory owners; and those in middle-class jobs, such as clerks, teachers and shopkeepers, also prospered in Britain's fast-growing economy. However, the poor remained very poor – often living in overcrowded back-to-back terraces of workers' housing built by the mill and factory bosses to be near to the factories. Those that worked in factories and mills often did so in appalling working conditions and working very long hours. (See the notes and accompanying photocopiable texts on 'Child labour in a mine', 'Inside a mine' and 'Child labour in a mill' in the Victorian Britain chapter.)

Discussing the picture

▶ Ask the children what they think this building is and whether they have seen any like this locally. What are they used for today? (Museums, offices, apartments, shopping centres.)

▶ Explain that in many parts of the north of England in Victorian times, large mills were built for spinning and weaving wool and cotton. Tell the children where this mill was built. Mention that in some places, as in Macclesfield, there were silk mills too.

▶ Talk about why mills were situated where they were, near to coalfields and transport links.

▶ Consider the changes that might be seen in localities like these, for example lots of cheap housing, railways, tall chimney stacks, smoke.

▶ Discuss how the effect of these mills was both positive and negative. They encouraged many thousands of people to crowd into towns like Manchester to look for work in the mills, they changed the physical geography of towns and cities and the social geography of villages, they created pollution, they lowered the price of textiles and clothes as these were mass-produced for the first time, they stimulated trade with the wider world and helped the economy.

Activities

▶ If possible, take the class to visit an old mill, or the site of a mill. There are many excellent working mills in museums around the country, such as the woollen mill in Hebden Bridge, West Yorkshire; Styal cotton mill, Cheshire and the Silk Museum in Macclesfield. While at the museum or site, collect information and encourage the children to make notes and sketches and take photographs, where permitted, for later use.

▶ In groups, ask the children to write a letter asking for information packs from one of the museums associated with mills like these. Then ask them to organise their findings into a presentation for the rest of the class.

▶ Research how the building of mills and factories in the 19th century affected the area around them. If there is a mill or factory in your area, look at evidence of urbanisation in, for example, the type of housing nearby and when other buildings were built. Look at maps to compare the area before and after the mill or factory was built.

▶ Look at the photograph 'Child labour in a mill' and photocopiable page 29 in the Victorian Britain chapter. Find out about factory owners who tried to provide better conditions for the people who worked for them, such as the Cadbury and Rowntree families and Titus Salt.

Terraced houses

This street in London's Whitechapel is typical of terraced houses in inner-city areas in Victorian Britain. Because of the influx of people from the countryside into the towns in search of work in factories, mills and mines, cheap housing was urgently needed. Industry owners built terraces of workers' houses near to their factories. They were quickly and cheaply built and many families could be housed in a relatively small area, near to their place of work. The houses are characteristically built of brick, with tall sash windows and arched doorways. They had tall chimneys, since they would all have been heated with coal fires. Often, the house would be entered from one or two steps up from the street and there would sometimes be a passageway between some of the houses to allow access to the back lanes or yards. They typically had one room upstairs and one room downstairs or 'two up two down' in better off areas.

Many houses built at the end of the 18th century and the early 19th century could be unhealthy to live in, because they had no running water, drains or lavatories. They were also often overcrowded, with many people sharing a room. The houses were made even more unhealthy when they were built back to back, leaving little opportunity for light or air to enter them. In 1848, the first Public Health Act was passed, but little was actually done to improve conditions. It was not until the 1870s that legislation began to take effect and significant progress was made. In late Victorian times, a great deal of new house building was undertaken in order to improve the living conditions of the working classes.

Discussing the photograph

▶ Ask the children to guess when this photograph was taken. (About 1880 or 1890.) How can they tell? (Look at the clothes, the lack of traffic, the horse and cart.)

▶ Discuss what the picture shows, telling the children that the houses are called terraces or terraced houses. Notice how long the street is.

▶ Discuss what the bridge across the middle of the street would have been for. (Trains.)

▶ Look at all the tall chimneys and talk about how the houses would have been heated.

▶ Discuss the fact that this is quite a wide street, making it lighter and healthier for people to live in. Point out that there was also somewhere for children to play. Compare this street and its relative cleanliness to the cartoon of the slum in the Victorian Britain Resource Gallery.

▶ Look at the construction material of the road and ask children if they know what this type of surface was made from. (Cobbles.)

▶ Ask if any of the children live in similar houses or streets to these today, or if there are any in the local area.

Activities
▶ Organise a class walk around the locality focusing on the older streets, particularly any Victorian terraces that remain in the area. As they walk around, ask the children to use 'Features of Victorian buildings' on photocopiable page 51 as a survey sheet to help them notice particular features. If possible, provide diagrams or picture examples of the items on the sheet. If appropriate, look out too for larger Victorian buildings, such as detached houses and the country houses or villas of factory owners, which may now be hotels or apartment buildings. Ask the children to note and sketch characteristic features.

▶ Back in the classroom, ask the children to make their own pictures or labelled diagrams of the Victorian houses they have seen. If appropriate, encourage them to use the word cards on photocopiable page 47 in any captions.

▶ Provide a floor plan for a Victorian house and/or a street plan for the children to study. Find the census data for the area covered and ask the children to find out about and note down significant information on the people who lived in these houses and what sort of occupations they had. Do they notice any trends?

▶ Look at street maps of a wider area to see how the streets were set out. Look at different parts of the locality to see if house building was concentrated in certain areas and whether some houses had more space around them. Look at the census data to see who might have lived in the larger houses.

▶ Ask the children to write about their findings for a Victorian class newspaper, reporting the building of new streets in the area and including illustrations of them.

Town hall

The Victorians were responsible for the building of many civic buildings in towns and cities across Britain. These buildings were intended to appear imposing and have many characteristic features. They often contained classical elements, such as Greek columns or facades, tall towers and the use of different coloured bricks to create designs. They were invariably decorated with intricate brickwork and carved woodwork to emphasise their importance in the community.

This modern photograph shows the town hall on the main street in Royal Leamington Spa, opened in 1884, and is an impressive example of a grand civic building. The overall classical effect is emphasised by the statue of Queen Victoria that stands in front of it.

Discussing the photograph
▶ Ask the children what kind of building they think this is. Look for clues that tell us it is an important building and if necessary tell the children that it is a town hall. Tell them when it was built and where it is.

▶ Talk about the features characteristic of Victorian times. Make reference to any terms on the word cards and 'Features of Victorian buildings' on photocopiable page 51.

▶ Ask the children if they can see any influences from another age, for example classical Greece and Rome. (The triangular-shaped additions on the front of the roof and the columns, for example, resemble the front of the Parthenon in Athens.)

▶ Note the different colours in the brickwork.

▶ Point out the statue of Victoria in the foreground, and discuss how this adds to the important, grand appearance of the building.

▶ Ask the children why the Victorians wanted to make these buildings so impressive.

▶ Discuss whether your own town has a town hall like this.

Activities
▶ Organise a class visit to the nearest town centre in the locality. Take sketching materials and cameras to survey any buildings that date from the Victorian period.

▶ Let the children use books, the Internet and the 'Features of Victorian buildings' on photocopiable page 51 to identify characteristic features of Victorian civic buildings in photographs. Ask the children to organise a display of their sketches.

▶ Make a collection of terms about Victorian buildings and make additions to the word cards on photocopiable page 47. Ask the children to make wordsearches and then exchange them with partners for them to work out.

▶ Suggest that the children work in small groups to research other examples of famous Victorian buildings, such as stations, follies, churches, hotels and villas.

NOTES ON THE PHOTOCOPIABLE PAGES

Word and sentence cards
PAGES 46–8

These cards build on vocabulary suggested by the QCA and include words and sentences related to:
▶ local history studies, such as *census*, *trade directory*, *locality*
▶ Victorian housing, such as *villa*, *terraced house*, *sash window*
▶ industrialisation, such as *factories*, *mines*, *mills*, *mechanisation*.

Encourage the children to think of other appropriate words to add to those provided, in order to build up a word bank for their work on local history. They could include words encountered in their researches, such as *source* and *semi-detatched*, in relation to the methods they learn about and the material they discover in their search for information about their locality. They could also use the cards in displays and in extended writing, such as in descriptive, factual and creative work and in writing discussions and arguments. The sentence cards suggest ways of using key words to summarise what they have learned.

Activities
▶ Once you have made copies of the word cards, cut them out and laminate them. They could be used for word games and spelling games, and for children to invent their own games.
▶ Make displays of the resources that have been used and use the word and sentence cards to label and describe them.
▶ Encourage the children to use the words in stories and non-fiction writing as often as possible.
▶ Make wordsearches and crossword puzzles for the children to complete using specific sets of words related to Victorian local history, such as words to do with different aspects of social change.
▶ Make cloze procedure sheets. Encourage the children to write the missing key words without support.
▶ Devise '20 questions' and 'Hangman' games based on the word cards.

Guidelines for local history research
PAGE 49

This set of guidelines is divided into paragraphs giving background information and advice about each type of basic source the children could use for their research on local history. Specific guidance is provided about how to use the different sources, such as avoiding copying out wholesale from books and printing large chunks of information from the Internet. Some questions are suggested, which children could ask themselves when deciding on the usefulness of sources such as pictures. The value of finding pictures of the same place from different periods in the past is also pointed out.

This is probably going to be an unusual type of text for some of the children to use and they may need guidance in ways of using it, for example as a 'help sheet' to have on hand when carrying out their research.

Discussing the text
▶ Ask the children what kind of text this is and what it is intended for.
▶ Ask them what the different paragraphs tell them.
▶ Point out that some of the paragraphs talk about what not to do. Why is this?
▶ Find volunteers to talk about the different kinds of sources they have used previously. Encourage them to talk about which of these is easiest to use and why.
▶ Discuss why it is important to use different sources. For example, to corroborate or substantiate the information found.
▶ Ask individuals to talk about the things they like to look up and how they like to work.
▶ See if the children enjoy working on their own at their own research. Encourage them to talk about why they find this enjoyable.
▶ Explain what they are learning by doing their own research, for example study skills, how to work independently, how to make their own decisions about what is useful or important, taking responsibility for their own learning (which is something that will stay with them for the rest of their lives).

Activities

▶ Before the children begin to work independently, model some of the research skills that they will be using, such as scanning a page or paragraph for useful information, selecting key words and noting key ideas. Work through some examples of how text can be written in your own words.

▶ Work with the whole class to devise a wide range of questions that they could keep in mind when choosing their sources, using those given in the text as examples.

▶ Make a collection of sources to include the types discussed. Divide the class into six groups and ask each group to work on a different type of source. Once they have found useful information and made some notes, ask a representative from each group to talk briefly to the class about their findings.

How to use census returns   PAGE 50

This text aims to explain what the census is and some ways of using it. The census is a source of central importance in local history, and the explanation hopes to show the children what a great deal of useful information about the past it contains. One way of engaging children in the idea of its importance might be to find some census data for the streets that they themselves live in, so that they can find out who may have lived in their street or even their house in the past.

The text points out that the census can be difficult to use, and they will need to be patient and hard working to find information, especially if they are using data printed on paper. If possible, try to ensure the census you want the children to use is available on a computer programme, such as Access, Excel or a school database, like Black Cat. Very able children could be expected to look for less obvious things in the data as extension work, such as the trends that the census shows.

Discussing the text

▶ Read through the text with the class and ask the children what kind of text this is.

▶ Ask them why it has been organised into paragraphs.

▶ Discuss ways in which the text might be used, such as guidelines while they use the census, or a starting point for developing their own questions and ideas.

▶ Explain how often a census is taken and why it is taken.

▶ Use a census return as an example in conjunction with this text. Ideally, show it to the class on a large screen or whiteboard. Look through each of the fields and ensure they know what the figures and words mean.

▶ Ask some simple questions about the data shown to illustrate how information can be found from the census. For example, *Who lived in…? Where was Mr … born?*

Activities

▶ Use an extract from your local census, choosing the streets where the children mostly live. Ask them to browse through it at first to see what kind of information it contains. Then ask the children to find their own street and, if possible, their own house. They can then see who lived there, what kind of family they may have been and the kind of jobs they may have done.

▶ Set the children a homework task of finding out about their own household. Ask the children to prepare an outline of a census return and to complete it at home, for their own house. In school, they can compare the information they have about their own house with that from an earlier census return. (If it proves difficult to provide exactly the census data that is needed for comparison, use data from a similar area.)

Features of Victorian buildings   PAGE 51

This sheet lists some of the key features of different kinds of Victorian buildings, from small homes to extravagant residences and public places. It incorporates building characteristics that can easily be seen and identified. The text can be read and discussed in class, but it also has use as an observation schedule, or survey sheet, that could be used when children are out on a local history walk. The features they notice could be ticked off, or perhaps sketched. It could be used in a similar way while children work in class on illustrations and photographs, books or material from the CD.

Local history word cards

census

census return

data

trade directory

street directory

locality

Census returns and directories are useful for finding out about people who lived in our locality in Victorian times.

Victorian housing word cards

villa
terraced house
workhouse
sash window
bargeboards
gable
Victorian terraced houses were built with sash windows.

Industrialisation word cards

factories
mines
mills
mechanisation
urbanisation
railway stations
canals
public health
When thousands of people moved to the cities to work in the factories and mills, it led to rapid urbanisation and problems with public health.

Guidelines for local history research

Using books

The first places to look for something in a reference book are the contents and index pages. The contents page will tell you what each chapter or section is about and may be the quickest way to find general information. If you have a key word you want to find out about, the index, arranged alphabetically, will list the page numbers where details can be found. If there is a range of pages on the topic, there is likely to be more information about it on these pages than on single pages. Some indexes show the important pages by using italic or bold.

When you have found a useful page, it will not be helpful to copy out exactly what is there. Scan for your key words and skim the paragraphs for useful information. Then re-read particular sections carefully. Notice additional key phrases or sentences and make a note of these. When you have noted all the key points, write out what you have found in your own words, organising your work in paragraphs.

Using pages on the Internet

It is not always helpful to simply print out pages from the Internet. Once you have found a useful page in a particular website, think of a key word or phrase that you want to know about. Click on *Edit* from the toolbar. Select *Find* and type your key word in the pop-up window. When you press *Enter* or click on *Find next*, the computer will find the word you want immediately. You can then read that small part of the text and use it as if it were on a page in a book, making notes as suggested above. You can use the find tool to search for your key word every time it appears on the web page.

Using pictures

Pictures, in various forms, often contain useful information about a topic. Skim through books and look for images when you use the Internet. When you have found a relevant picture, ask some questions about it, such as 'What does this tell me about Victorian Manchester?' 'What has changed since this picture was taken?' If you can find images of a place from different periods, the comparison can be a very useful way of seeing changes.

Oral history

This is a very important source for local history. When a person talks about their memories they are providing oral history. For an interview, work out in advance what topics you want the person to talk about. You can always add extra questions as you go along. Note down what the person says. This can then be written up as an 'oral history record'.

Other sources

Useful information can be had from maps, plans, census data, directories, newspapers, diaries, letters and stories among other things. These sources tell us different things that we can piece together to form an idea of what it was like in the past.

How to use census returns

What are census returns?

These are tables full of information about people who lived in different areas of the country. The census began in 1801 and has been carried out every ten years since then (except 1941). It is a way of counting the population of the country and finding out what all the people did. The first really reliable census was not made until 1851. The information on the returns (the forms filled in and returned to the data collectors) is organised under particular headings, or 'fields', which include *name of person*, *number of house*, *street*, *male/female*, *occupation*, *where born*. All this data is organised according to streets.

What can I find out from them?

The returns can tell us who lived in a particular house, for example in 1851; what their occupation was, where they were born and how many other people lived in the house. You can find out how many children there were in the family and who their neighbours were. By looking at the same street on another date, you can find out who lived in the same house years later.

Is the census a hard source to use?

If the census data is in the original, old-fashioned writing, it will be difficult to read, and if it is on sheets of paper, it will take a long time to find the information you may want. Many schools now have census data on their computer systems. If this has been done, you will not find it hard to use at all. Look on the field that you want and highlight, for example, one of the *scholars*. Then click on *Filter* and the computer will find and count all the school children for you. You can find out who they were, their ages and where they lived.

You could also search for a particular family by highlighting their surname and filtering. You will then find where they lived, how many family members there were, their names, ages and so on. You could see whether they were rich and lived in a large house with servants or by themselves in a small house. You could find out a great deal of information about one person from a careful search of the census.

What other things can it be used for?

The census is useful for finding changes. If you look at where people were born and where they later worked, for example in 1851, you can compare this with the same information from a later date, such as 1891. You might find that in 1891, people travelled much further to find jobs than they did before rail travel was widely available.

Features of Victorian buildings

Terraces
▶ No gardens at the front
▶ Door opens onto the street, sometimes with steps
▶ Curved pattern in bricks of a different colour over the door
▶ Sash windows
▶ Tall chimneys
▶ Back yard, or alleyway between rows of houses

Large detached or semi-detached town houses
▶ Front garden with railings or fence
▶ Porch and arched doorway
▶ Very tall windows
▶ Three or four storeys
▶ Gables, often with bargeboards
▶ Several tall chimneys with pots in patterned brick
▶ Patterned ridge tiles on the roof

Country houses or villas
▶ Sometimes incorporates style from the past, such as 17th century or classical Greece or Rome
▶ Very large, tall chimneys with twisting brick patterns on the pots
▶ Large windows
▶ Imposing driveways and entrances

▶ Large grounds, sometimes with formal gardens and a kitchen garden of vegetables and fruit

Large public buildings, such as town halls, concert halls and libraries
▶ Tall towers, spires and gables; sometimes domes
▶ Classical columns and porticoes
▶ Detailed brickwork in contrasting colours, particularly red and yellow
▶ Impressive entrances up steps, through tall, wide doorways
▶ Intricate archways and many tall gothic windows
▶ Stone balconies
▶ Ornate facades
▶ Statue at front, often of Queen Victoria

Churches
▶ Tall steeples
▶ Steeply sloping roofs
▶ Gothic windows and doorways
▶ Intricate brickwork
▶ Sometimes using the style of Ancient Greek temples
▶ Colonnades including Ionic and Corinthian columns
▶ Greek-style statues

BRITAIN SINCE 1948

Content, skills and concepts

This chapter relates to unit 13 of the QCA Scheme of Work and will assist in planning and resourcing work on Britain since 1948. It is assumed that this unit will be taught mainly to Years 5 or 6, and may also be adapted for earlier age groups. It suggests ways of investigating change in Britain and the reasons for and results of those changes. Children develop their understanding of the period, including the characteristics and diversity of popular culture. They learn to make links between changes within the period and apply their skills of historical enquiry to their study of the recent past.

Together with the Britain Since 1948 Resource Gallery on the CD-ROM, this chapter introduces a range of sources, including contemporary photographs. It addresses the question *How has life in Britain changed since 1948?*, focusing particularly on fashion, communication and immigration. The chapter also provides material to support the teaching of key historical concepts relevant to this period.

Children will already have gained experience of sequencing and using timelines, using time-related vocabulary, asking and answering questions, and using written, visual and auditory sources. Recounting stories about the past, and looking for similarities and differences between the past and the present are prior learning activities that will have introduced relevant skills and concepts to the children before they progress to the skills and concepts in this unit. This chapter includes suggestions for the extension of these and other skills, such as recognising change and continuity and the ability to select and use information to support a discussion.

Resources on the CD-ROM

Contemporary and recent photographs, and maps of the Empire and Commonwealth are provided on the CD-ROM, along with two interviews. Background information about these sources is provided in the teacher's notes, with ideas for further work on them.

Photocopiable pages

Photocopiable resources at the end of the chapter (and also in PDF format on the CD) include:
▶ word cards that highlight the essential vocabulary of this topic
▶ a timeline
▶ statistics on population changes
▶ texts on immigration and other changes to life since 1948.

The teacher's notes that accompany the photocopiable pages include suggestions for developing discussion and for using them for whole class, group or individual activities. Within the photocopiable texts, topic-specific vocabulary is introduced. This includes words associated with the study of Britain since 1948 and changes to life since then, such as in population, home amenities and welfare. There are tables showing population increase and the places of birth of immigrants during the period, first-hand accounts by Jamaican immigrants and comment on the introduction of the National Health Service.

The texts can be used for shared or guided reading, and more able children may be able to read them independently. The tables of statistics will provide a useful link of the application of number to a real-life context.

History skills

Skills such as observation, description, the use of time-related vocabulary, understanding the meaning of dates, comparing, inferring, listening, speaking, reading, writing and drawing are involved in the activities suggested.

Historical understanding

A further aim is for children to develop more detailed knowledge of the past and their ability to sequence and date events independently, through their understanding of the context and content of factual information. They will begin to give reasons for events and use primary sources to find further information. They will also have the opportunity to extend their skills in using descriptive and time-related language in writing their own accounts of the past.

NOTES ON THE CD-ROM RESOURCES

The British Empire in 1901

Britain's industrialisation during the 19th century meant that factory owners and manufacturers were able to look abroad for materials. Increased production capacity and export links also meant that they were able to look for new markets in which to sell the products manufactured in British factories. Britain was keen to protect its new markets against competition from other countries and this led to Britain taking control of many areas of the world that were useful for trade. As well as stopping these states trading with other countries, Britain was able to gain new land for British people to live in.

By Edward VII's reign (1901–1910), Britain had the largest empire the world had seen. It included Canada, India and what was to become Pakistan, islands in the far east such as North Borneo, New Guinea and Hong Kong, Australia, New Zealand, colonies in Africa, islands in the Caribbean and Pacific and some parts of South America.

The Commonwealth in 2003

In 1931, Parliament passed the Statute of Westminster, which set up the British Commonwealth, an organisation that recognised Britain and the dominions as equal partners. This happened as a result of the demands for greater independence and self-government from Canada, South Africa, Australia and New Zealand. At that time, the Irish Free State was also a member of the British Commonwealth.

After 1948, when colonial ties had begun to break down and the Empire began to be dismantled, newly independent states, such as India, Pakistan, Sri Lanka and Ghana, joined the Commonwealth and this enabled them to keep close ties with Britain.

By 1965, nearly all of the old British colonies in Africa had become independent and had decided to join the Commonwealth. South Africa had been temporarily expelled from the Commonwealth however (in 1961), because of its policy of apartheid. In 2003, the Commonwealth has 54 member countries, consisting of approximately 1.7 billion people – 30% of the world's population.

Discussing the maps

▶ Ask the children to look carefully at the map of the British Empire in 1901. Suggest they read the key and discuss what the shadings mean.

▶ Find volunteers to name some of the large areas and countries that were part of the Empire.

▶ Ask anyone who has travelled to or lived in any of these places to talk about their experiences.

▶ Tell the children how the Empire developed and that people went from Britain to live in these countries.

▶ Talk about why people may have had to live abroad, such as their work in the army or government, and why some chose to live in another country.

▶ Establish the meanings of the words *Empire* and *emigration*.

▶ Now ask the children to look carefully at the map of the Commonwealth. Discuss the significance of the pink areas.

▶ Ask volunteers to name the countries or areas that are part of the Commonwealth today.

▶ Discuss the meaning of the term *Commonwealth*. Ask the children to split the compound word into its two parts and then consider its meaning. Help them to appreciate the idea of a community of shared interests and mutual benefit.

▶ Ask the children what they may already know about the Commonwealth, for example from the Commonwealth Games.

▶ Explain to the children how the Commonwealth was created and why.

▶ Consider the change in attitude between Empire and Commonwealth. Ask the children what they think the advantages might be that encourage countries to join the Commonwealth.

▶ Discuss the reasons why South Africa was expelled from the Commonwealth for many years (between 1961 and 1994). Talk about attitudes to equality and explain that laws are in place in most Commonwealth countries to make sure that people are treated fairly and equally. More recently, Zimbabwe was suspended because of its human rights violations.

▶ Ask the children if they have heard of other countries that have begun to group together, and why they are doing this. (For example, the European Union.)

Activities

▶ Help the children to locate the dates of the two maps on a class timeline. They could also add significant dates, such as the formation of the Commonwealth in 1931.

▶ Provide the children with a two-column chart to list the countries in the Empire in 1901 and those in the present day Commonwealth. They can then note the differences in the two lists and suggest why there have been changes.

▶ Ask the children to write an explanation text about why the Commonwealth was formed.

▶ Challenge the children to select a Commonwealth country and make a diagram of information about its people, geography, religion and history.

1940s suit

This photograph, taken in about 1942, shows smart 'utility wear' for women. During the Second World War, every type of cloth, as well as labour and other materials, was in short supply and strict rationing was introduced in Britain in 1941 (not lifted until 1949). Specially made items were produced for people to buy with coupons from their ration books. It was considered unpatriotic and selfish for people to wear fussy, elaborate styles, since this was considered a waste of precious resources and inappropriate to the mood of the time. Styles of women's tailoring tended to be 'sensible', austere, and in dark, serviceable colours, often taking style cues from men's and women's military uniforms. Fabrics were hard wearing. Detail and ornamentation were not permitted on the specially made garments, restrictions applying even down to the number of buttons allowed. Although following these practical designs with a simple pleat in the skirt, this suit is smart, has a subtle check and a flattering fitted shape.

1950s flower-print dress

Ladies clothing styles in the 1950s portrayed a reaction against the austerity of wartime dress. As the country began to become more prosperous following the Second World War, more people could afford to dress more extravagantly and individually, and were keen to do so after the hardships and sobriety of the war. Clothing trends in the early 1950s reflected the move away from stiff, sober practicality of dress during the war and women felt able to be brighter in their appearance and grooming.

Two styles were particularly prominent for women at this time – the pencil skirt, which was straight and quite tight, and full skirts, which were often made to look fuller by wearing layers of stiff net underskirts. Neither style was always comfortable to wear, particularly as most women still wore girdles. The difference between the styles was reflected in the range of fabrics and patterns that also started to be used, including the light fabric and bold, flowery, feminine pattern shown in the example in this summer photograph.

Stiletto heels became fashionable on shoes, along with pointed toes. Shoes came in many bright colours, with white being a favourite. Light chiffon headscarves were a popular accessory to keep hairstyles tidy. Bright make-up and large sunglasses were also fashionable and freely available.

1960s mini-dress

The feeling of exuberance and openness caused by a booming economy marked the towns and cities of Britain in the 1960s, and this was reflected in women's fashion. People no longer wanted to be bound by rigid dress codes and the young in particular wanted to wear what they liked. Fashions became more flamboyant with bold prints and patterns being used for both men and women's clothes, later designs often taking an Eastern influence. Most notably, the 1960s was the era in which the miniskirt was created by Mary Quant, and many skirts and dresses were designed to be as short as possible. Some of these mini-dresses were designed in 'psychedelic' patterns and colours. Big chequer-board patterns of black and white and other monochrome designs were also popular.

This girl from the 1960s wears a simple, black, polo-neck mini-dress and black, patent knee boots. Her hair is long and free and she has quite thick, dark eye make-up, but paler lips. Because of the length of skirts, stockings were discarded in favour of tights and young women no longer wore girdles. Heavy jewellery and long hairstyles or distinctive, chunky, asymmetrical hairstyles also became popular. These hair designs were often simpler and more naturally maintained than the highly coiffured, sprayed and pinned ones from the 40s and 50s.

1970s flared jeans

The end of the 1960s and the 1970s saw the British economy begin to slow and a reaction against the materialism of the late 1950s and early 1960s. Young people were leading the way in looking for alternative ways of living and taking inspiration from other cultures. These trends, along with the hippie movement, influenced fashion. Skirts were often worn very long, clothes became loser and more free flowing, often worn in layers. Influences from India and the East meant that natural, 'basic' fabrics such as cheesecloth and crocheted wool became popular, and simple jewellery like strings of long beads were also worn. Shoes tended to be either platform-soled or wedge-heeled. Both men and women often grew their hair long and accessorised the styles with colourful headbands.

This photograph shows an example of more mainstream fashion of the time. The model has adopted a North American 'country' look – a variation on a romantic theme made popular in the 1970s by designers such as Laura Ashley. She wears stiff, tight jeans that flare widely from the knee. High-heeled platform shoes with buckle straps and contrasting soles are worn beneath these wide bottomed trousers. Here, the gingham shirt with a tied waist completes the country image. Hairstyles were long and informal in appearance but, as part of an overall image like this one, were often carefully flicked and curled.

The end of the 1970s saw the rise of punk and new wave trends, reflecting young people's social and domestic rebellion. Punk particularly cultivated a provocative and angry look, with spiky hair dyed in bright colours; tight clothes and slogan-sprayed T-shirts. Tartan and PVC fabrics were popular, with accessories such as chains, safety pins and studded dog collars.

1980s dungarees

By the 1980s, some clothing styles had become even more relaxed. However, women had fought to enter the workplace on an equal basis with men and their clothes reflected that change in outlook. Office wear for women moved towards 'power dressing' with formal, tailored suits consisting of short skirts and shoulder-padded jackets. Casual wear often reflected a 'sporty' look, with an emphasis on comfort. Brightly coloured leggings and tracksuits became popular everyday wear.

Here is an example of one style of young people's casual wear: a simple, grey-marl T-shirt worn with pale denim dungarees, inspired by manual labourers' workwear and having a somewhat unisex feel. Chunky boots, particularly made by Dr Martens, usually accompanied an outfit like this. Jeans were hugely popular across many age and social groups. Layering was also fashionable, so sweatshirts and casual jackets were sometimes worn loosely over other garments. Jewellery tended to be big and chunky, and wearing a large number of bangles and leather wrist thongs was a trendy look. Lacy scarves and ribbons were a trend from the New Romantic movement. A popular style of women's hair in the 1980s was big and layered, often back-combed to stand up off the face with a slightly rough, unstyled look (although the power dressers would have much smoother, more precise styles). To contrast these 'unfeminine', workwear style points, long, sparkly earrings are worn and the bright pink blusher and lipstick exaggerates feminine features.

Discussing the photographs

▶ Set up the five pictures as a slideshow from the CD-ROM.

▶ Discuss the clues that tell us each one is a photograph from the past and ask the children if they can suggest in which era each photograph was taken.

▶ As you talk about each photograph in turn, explain a little bit about what was going on in the world during the decade. For example, with the 1940s picture, mention how long the war had been going on by the time the picture was taken in 1942.

▶ Discuss the style and shape of the clothes and think about what may have influenced this. (For example, the military look of the 1940s, the more carefree image of the 1950s.) Ask the children to suggest why these styles would have been popular during these different times.

▶ Discuss what else they notice about the clothes. Discuss whether girls and young women would like to wear clothes like these now. What kind of clothing is popular these days?

▶ Explain to the children about the need for 'utility wear' in the 1940s and what this meant in terms of comfort and style.

▶ Find volunteers to point to the practical features of the 1940s suit that they can see. (For example, the plainness, the lack of unnecessary detail, the heavyweight cloth.)

▶ Ask the children to comment on main changes in 1950s dress compared with the 1940s.
▶ Discuss the most dramatic change that has taken place in ladies' fashions in the 1960s.
▶ Ask the children to identify the characteristic style shown in the 1970s picture, and talk about what has influenced this style. (For example, the outdoor life, a casual look.)
▶ Ask the children to comment on the style in the 1980s photograph, and to comment on the influences on this style, such as common types of clothing for men and women, possibly resulting from changes in attitudes and the passing of the Sex Discrimination Act (1975).

Activities

▶ Look at the timeline of Britain since 1948 (photocopiable page 75). Ask the children to note how it is subdivided. Explain the meaning of *decade* if necessary. Ask the children to make a timeline of the decade of their own life span. This could be completed at home with the help of parents or carers.
▶ Compare the fashion styles shown in the pictures across all five decades, and provide other visual examples if possible (perhaps from films, television programmes, books and magazines). Ask the children to point out key changes they can see. See if they notice any patterns in the changes, for example fashion gradually becomes more relaxed, informal and comfortable. Revise the meaning of the term *trend* and how this gives rise to *trendy*. Remind the children that trends can be seen in many areas of life, not just those to do with clothes fashion. Ask them to devise a chart to show trends in ladies' fashions in Britain since 1948.
▶ Help the children to draw a sequence of pictures showing trends in the fashions of boys and girls of their age over the last few decades.
▶ Ask the children to write a short information text about why utility wear was introduced during the Second World War, first identifying the different reasons, such as patriotism, practicality, lack of materials and resources.
▶ Organise the children into groups to find out about influential fashion designers in Britain, such as Norman Hartnell, Mary Quant, Laura Ashley, Vivienne Westwood and Paul Smith. Ask them to make a presentation of their findings to the rest of the class.
▶ Ask the children to identify clothing aspects that characterised particular decades and add them to enlarged copies of the timeline on photocopiable page 75.
▶ Help the children to find out about men's fashion in each of the decades and make a display which shows how men and women's fashion changed over the five decades. Add brief captions that highlight some of the major historical events of the decades.

1940s telephone

In many ways, this old telephone handset looks very similar to phones that were used well into the 1970s (see the '1960s telephone' also on the CD), with a similar boxy shape, large, bulbous receiver and round dial (and extendable spring-shaped cord that is still used today). However, the phone in this picture would have felt quite heavy, since it was made from an early kind of plastic, called Bakelite. Bakelite plastics and resins were used to make many household items in the 1930s and 40s. There would also have been a mechanical metal bell fitted inside the telephone in order to make the ringing sound. Although many modern digital phones are shaped like mobile phones, the main difference between this 1950s phone and a modern one is that it used a circular dial for entering the number you wanted to call. (This is where the verb 'to dial' a number comes from.) Although some modern phones still include letters on the number buttons, today telephone numbers are numbers only, dialled using push buttons. In the 1940s and some years later, both letters and numbers were used, the letters often spelling out a word. These telephones were a typical style in the 1940s, and were nearly always made in black. Not many people had them in their homes at this stage.

Discussing the picture

▶ Ask if any volunteers could suggest a decade when this telephone was made and used.
▶ Talk about the features of the phone that are different from modern ones.
▶ Explain to the children that it would have been very heavy compared with a modern phone, and discuss the fact that it was made from Bakelite, an early, heavy, plastic material.
▶ Ask what other features tell us it is old, for example the dial, the letters, the style of the handset and body of the phone. Explain to the children, if necessary, that to dial a number the user would put a fingertip (or pencil) into the appropriate 'hole' on the dial and pull the dial clockwise until the finger reached the metal stop.

▶ Ask the children to think of other features that can't be seen that might make it old-fashioned, for example the bell.

▶ Look at the wording in the middle of the dial, and talk about what it implies. (That the communication technology needed did not work as instantly as it does today.)

Activities

▶ If possible, bring in an example of an old telephone of this type. Compare the old phone with a modern one and discuss the changes.

▶ Compare the use of the telephone in the 1940s with that of the modern mobile phone (see 'Mobile phone' provided on the CD), and discuss the advantages and disadvantages of the two. (For example, clarity, more reliance on a central operator to connect calls, use over long distances, the way they are powered.) Although public call boxes may have been less numerous in the 40s, they were probably more widely used, since people did not generally have telephones of their own. (See Jack's comments on this in the interview 'How life has changed since 1948', provided on the CD.) Give the children a two-column grid to write down their comparisons, and conclude by discussing which is considered more or less useful.

▶ Talk about the importance of the telephone during the war. Discuss who would have used it most – perhaps those who had suffered injuries or property damage during the bombing.

1960s telephone

The material for this telephone is a more modern plastic, probably in greys or browns, but the basic style has changed little from that of the 1940s. It still rings using a conventional bell, and it still has a dial for entering the number to be called. Telephone numbers and codes were still a combination of letters and numbers. One small design improvement to be noted, however, is that the letters and numbers are now placed outside the dialling circle, so that they can be seen more easily while dialling. This change was probably made to facilitate the dialling process, because with the increase in usage, telephone numbers were much longer. By the 1960s more people had their own phones in their houses, but it was still far from being the case that everyone had their own phone.

Discussing the photograph

▶ Ask the children when they think this telephone dates from.

▶ Ask them to compare it with the telephone from the 1940s, noting the major differences. Notice how there are many similarities.

▶ Discuss what the children think is the most significant change or the most useful one.

▶ Compare this phone with a modern one, and note how many more considerable changes have been made since the 1960s.

Activities

▶ Provide the children with data about the technological developments of communication in the second half of the 20th century. Ask them to make notes during their research, looking for causes and effects of improved and new types of communication, and then write up a carefully structured piece, drawing towards some conclusions they can make from the data.

▶ Ask the children to identify key points in the development of the telephone, making notes and collecting and drawing pictures of telephones at different points in this process. Ask them to consider recent developments such as satellite and cable supplies and use of the Internet. Finally help the children to produce a timeline of telephones.

▶ Talk about some of the people involved in the development of personal communications, such as Edison, Bell, Marconi, Baird. Challenge the children to find further information about these people for homework and to write up captions for the timeline.

Mobile phone

The mobile phone is based on portable wireless technology. This technology enables phones to be completely portable, as they work without using landlines or cables. Telephone companies were unable to make use of this technology in full for many years because of the shortage of communication channels. This problem was solved with the introduction of cellular technology, which increased the number of transmitters available in certain geographical areas. During the 1990s and early 2000s, mobile phone technology improved at a pace, away from the unreliable, cumbersome, almost brick-sized models of the 1980s. Phones became smaller and smaller and began to offer more and more facilities, such as texting, games, an alarm clock, an endless variety of ring-tones, the option to vibrate instead of ring, hands-free kits, Internet links, even video-phones and, as the phone in this picture is able to do, take and send digital photographs.

A mobile phone has become something of a fashion accessory as well as a communication tool, particularly with young people and older children and because rapid technological developments mean more advanced models are coming out all the time. There are a wide variety of different shapes, styles and colours, payment packages and accessories. Although the number of manufacturers and network suppliers is fairly small, the number of mobile phone retailers increased enormously during the late 1990s and early 2000s, giving a very different look to the average high street.

Discussing the photograph
▶ Ask the children to tell you what this photograph shows.
▶ Establish who the manufacturer of the phone is and in which part of the world the company is based. (South-East Asia.)
▶ Ask the children what is special about this particular mobile phone.
▶ Talk about how mobile phones were initially quite large and heavy, and how now they have become so much smaller and lighter. Think about why this is.
▶ Discuss how mobile phones work, compared with mainline phones. (For example, they do not need lines or cables.)
▶ Explain how mobile phones are powered by battery-cell technology and tell the class about how cellular phones need transmitters that can be placed where they are needed using tall masts. Discuss the effect of all these transmitter masts on the environment and why many people have said they do not want them. Consider why this is. (For example, fear of low-level radiation emissions.)

Activities
▶ Set the children the task of carrying out a simple survey for homework into the number of people they know who use mobile phones. Suggest they make a tally chart and bring their findings back to school for discussion and to compare with the others in the class.
▶ Provide the children with photographs of mobile phone masts and mobile phone stores. Ask them to write about the changes that are taking place in their local area.
▶ Hold a class debate about the amount of mobile phone masts that have sprung up around the country, and include discussion about the number that have been put up near schools.

Early computer

This is a photograph taken in 1943 of the 'Colossus' computer, the world's first programmable electronic computer. It was housed at Bletchley Park in Buckinghamshire, the intelligence centre of the British forces during the Second World War. Colossus was used to help in breaking the Enigma codes used in secret communications between Hitler and his armed forces, which the Germans considered to be unbreakable.

What is amazing today is the massive size of the computer. Although less complex than modern ones and with fewer capabilities, Colossus filled an entire room and needed more than one person to operate it. More recent technological advances have meant that all the equipment seen in this picture can be remade and fitted onto a microchip, making computer functions available in many more different contexts.

Discussing the photograph
▶ Initially, look at the photograph with the children without telling them what it is. Ask if anyone can work out what it might be, and then tell them that it is one of the first computers to have been built.
▶ Together, examine the features that make it so different from a modern computer.
▶ Explain that it was called Colossus, and discuss why this name was so appropriate.
▶ Tell the children about how it was used in the Second World War to break German secret communication codes. Explain how this vital breakthrough helped the Allies to win the war. Stress how expensive the machine was and how the technology was so new that it probably would not have been invented then if not for its need in the war.

▶ Look closely at all the plugs, valves, circuits and connections, and discuss whether modern computers have fewer electrical components than this or just smaller ones. Discuss the term *micro-technology*, and talk about modern computer components being smaller but more powerful than early ones.

▶ Think about how Colossus would have been operated in comparison with the simple one-person keyboard and mouse functions of modern PCs.

Activities
▶ Ask the children to place Colossus on the timeline on photocopiable page 75. They could also research the development of computers and create their own computer timeline.

▶ Provide a range of books and suitable web pages, including www.bletchleypark.org.uk, and ask the children to search for further information about Colossus and the work of the researchers at Bletchley Park. The children could then write their own account of why Colossus was important.

▶ If appropriate, organise a visit to Retrobeep, the computer museum at Bletchley Park, where most of the exhibits are operational.

Laptop computer

The light, slim, highly portable facilities of this modern laptop are made possible by the development of micro technology, and by the creation of the flat screen which is used as a monitor. Created near the end of the 20th century, the laptop is for personal use. It folds almost flat and can be carried easily in a small case. The great advantage of these small computers is that they have all the facilities and capabilities of a much larger, desk-based PC, but can be used virtually anywhere. Some modern trains, for example, have computer ports by the seats where a laptop can be plugged in, so that people can continue to work while travelling. A laptop also contains a battery, which enables it to be used without being connected to an external power source, needing only a telephone line if Internet access is needed.

Discussing the photograph
▶ Look at the photograph of the laptop computer, and discuss why it is called by this name.
▶ Discuss what types of people are likely to use laptops, and what they are used for.
▶ Compare this miniaturised technology with Colossus and older, more cumbersome office computers. Ask if anyone can explain any of the affects these changes have had. (For example, smaller components meant the whole computer could be smaller and more manageable. This in turn meant that it could fit into a smaller space and be used in offices and eventually in people's homes. This led to higher sales and cheaper computers which, nowadays, many people can afford to buy for themselves.)
▶ Discuss the modern uses of computers and the wide range of things they are used for. Consider how many functions of work, home and school life now rely on computer technology and how different this has made certain aspects of life compared with 30 or 40 years ago.

Activities
▶ Compare the photograph of the laptop with that of the Colossus computer. Ask for volunteers to point out the major differences. Discuss some of the modern uses of computers (for example for business and leisure), and compare these with the role of Colossus during the war.

▶ Challenge the children to find out how the computer has developed and changed. Working in pairs or small groups, they could summarise their findings in a variety of ways, for example in a timeline, a chart, a sequence of pictures, or a written summary.

▶ Discuss the wide range of things that computer technology can now be used for. For a homework activity, ask the children to list all the items in their home that use computer-based technology, for example mobile phone, video/DVD player, washing machine possibly, some of their toys, games consoles, microwave oven.

▶ Help the children to find out about some key people involved in the invention and development of the computer, such as Alan Turing, Eckert and Mauchly, Bill Gates, Stephen Wozniak, Clive Sinclair. Ask them, in groups, to write a short biography of one of these for inclusion in a display or class book about computers.

▶ Conduct a school survey to find out how many computers are owned at home, and whether they are PCs, laptops or another type, such as an iMac. Ask the children to create a simple database of their results. Then use graphing programs to show the results in a suitable form.

The Empire Windrush

In 1948, partly at the invitation of the British government, this ship brought 530 people from Jamaica to England. They had left their homes in search of better jobs and improved prospects. This was only one group among many that arrived in Britain from the Caribbean, as well as from different colonial countries around the world after the war. Many of the people from the Caribbean had never been to Britain before and felt extremely excited and nervous about their arrival in a country very different from their own. Some, however, were quite familiar with Britain and its people, having lived here during the war while working as members of the armed services. Many men from the West Indies had served as RAF pilots during the war.

Immigrants from the Caribbean

This photograph shows some of the newly arrived Caribbean immigrants at Tilbury Docks in London. Mostly ex-RAF servicemen, these men had been encouraged here to escape unemployment at home. Many were skilled and highly qualified, but were anxious about what kind of work they would find in Britain. At first, they were accommodated in hostels in London, but then they had to find work and homes of their own. Often, they were not accepted by the local population and were denied work at a level for which they were qualified. Many had to take very low paid jobs as cleaners or porters on the railways and in hospitals. Despite this difficult beginning, many immigrant families succeeded in their aim of a better life and are among the high achievers, contributing greatly to the country's wealth and culture.

Discussing the pictures

▶ Look at the first photograph and ask a volunteer to read the inscription on the ship. Ask if anyone has heard of this famous ship before.

▶ Encourage them to explain why they think it is well known and still remembered today. (It was the first ship to bring large numbers of immigrants from the Caribbean islands.)

▶ Explain briefly some of the history of the *Windrush*. Tell the children why it was such a significant event. The 530 immigrants that sailed on it could be seen as the catalyst for increasing immigration into Britain, which has led to some very wide-ranging changes in British society.

▶ Look at the second photograph and ask the children what they think is happening here.

▶ Discuss why the men are looking through the newspaper, and what they may be looking for, for example news of their own arrival, job vacancies.

▶ Look at how they are dressed. Speculate on whether some of them are wearing their best clothes and if so, why.

▶ Notice their expressions and imagine how they might have felt in this situation.

▶ Tell the class about the unwelcoming reception they often received, and the kind of jobs some of them eventually got.

▶ Explain briefly about the background of many of the *Windrush* passengers, for example they were professionals and people who had worked for Britain in the RAF.

▶ Mention that most of the immigrants around this time arrived in London, but their families later spread out to many areas of the country.

Activities

▶ Locate and label the arrival of the *Windrush* on the timeline on photocopiable page 75.

▶ Find out whether any of the relatives of the children in the class arrived on the *Windrush*. Suggest the children find out about the arrivals of other groups of immigrants (for example the 'brain drain' from Asia in the 1960s and 70s) and make an immigration timeline. They could also add emigrants to the timeline (for example the post-war migration boom to Australia).

▶ Ask the children to find the relative positions of Jamaica and England on a map to consider how far these people travelled.

▶ Discuss carefully the attitudes of many British people in the 1940s towards new arrivals. As well as simple prejudice, think about other reasons for their concerns, for example that immigrants might take their jobs. Ask the children to consider the kinds of jobs that immigrants and their descendants do now and the work they contribute to communities around the country. Their discussions should help them to conclude that people from immigrant families are involved in every sector of working life.

▶ Divide the class into groups to create a role-play activity based on the arrival of the *Windrush* immigrants. For example, talking about their hopes and fears; discussing what they thought it

would be like; planning how they will find jobs, homes and so on; what the journey was like; if they miss their home. (Use the accounts on photocopiable page 78 for ideas.)
▶ Ask the children to work in pairs or small groups to discuss what they can learn from the tables about population and immigration on photocopiable pages 76 and 77. Suggest they write simple statements to show interesting findings.

Immigrants from Kenya

This photograph shows a group of Asian-Africans disembarking at Gatwick from a flight from Kenya in 1968. Asians in East Africa came originally from India and Pakistan, but had settled in countries such as Kenya and Uganda during British rule and had worked hard to set up businesses. However, political changes in these countries meant that in 1967, many Kenyan Asians were forced to leave Kenya. In 1972, Ugandan Asians were expelled from Uganda. They were given 90 days to leave. Not long before they were expelled, legislation had been passed in this country to end automatic entitlement for Commonwealth citizens to settle in Britain. However, in the case of these Asian-Africans, those with British passports were allowed to enter as refugees.

Discussing the photograph
▶ Talk about what is happening in this photograph and where it is taking place.
▶ Give the children a bit of background about the events that led up to the expulsion of the Asians from Africa and tell them when it all happened.
▶ Ask the children to describe the expressions of the new arrivals and imagine how they may have felt. Do they look like they may have had little time to prepare for this new life?
▶ Think about where they have come from and what the climate change must have been like. Discuss whether their clothes look warm enough – has anyone got a coat? The blankets may have been handed out on the plane. Compare the way they are dressed – more suitable to their home – with the 'English' dress of the Jamaican immigrants. Does this suggest they were less prepared for their journey, that they are perhaps more reluctant migrants?
▶ If appropriate, include some simple discussion on the distinction between *immigrant* and *refugee*.
▶ Notice that this photograph shows women and children too, as whole families of Asian-Africans were forced to leave their homes.

Activities
See 'British passport holder' below.

British passport holder

This photograph shows a newly arrived Asian man from Kenya. He was one of the many Asians who fled Kenya and was able to enter Britain as a British passport holder. (At that time, as India was a former colony and member of the Commonwealth, Indians would have had British passports.) Soon after the arrival of people like these, the government introduced an emergency bill and, later, three successive Immigration Acts, passed in 1962, 1968 and 1971, aimed at restricting the number of immigrants from Commonwealth countries. This man arrived just in time to beat the new restrictions.

Large numbers of migrants also came from Bangladesh, India and Pakistan around the same time, but the number of people from these areas has increased greatly in recent times (see photocopiable page 77). Personal experiences are recalled in the interview with Mota Singh (provided on the CD), who arrived from India in the 1960s.

Discussing the photograph
▶ Explain that this man is one of the refugees from Africa who came to Britain in the late 1960s and early 1970s.
▶ Discuss why this man is seen holding up his passport. Ask the children why they think this was such an important document to him.
▶ Think about what he might do next, where he might go once he leaves the airport. Remind them of the discussions they had on the 'Immigrants from the Caribbean', if you have looked at that picture. Ask the children what they might do if they were in his position. For example, they might try to find some friends or family that are already in the new country.

Activities
► Help the children to locate and label the date of the arrival of the Kenyan and Ugandan Asians on the timeline on photocopiable page 75 and compare this with the arrival of those from Jamaica (see 'The Empire Windrush' and 'Immigrants from the Caribbean' on page 60).

► Use the maps of the Empire and Commonwealth provided on the CD to help the children identify the main areas from which immigrants came.

► Let the children research the social and political news of this period, especially events that happened in East Africa. Set the task of writing an imaginary letter to a relative in Britain asking if it will be possible to come and stay with them for a time, when they leave Kenya or Uganda.

► Set up a hot-seating situation, where you take on the role of the gentleman arriving with his passport. Let the children act in the role of journalists, asking you prepared questions. Allow the children some time to work in pairs or small groups to draw up their list of interview questions.

► Help the children to find out about other countries from which large numbers of refugees have come more recently, for example ethnic Albanians and others affected by the Kosovan/Balkan conflicts, Iraq, Zimbabwe, Somalia, Afghanistan.

Interview: Immigration

In this video, Mota Singh talks about his experiences as an immigrant in the 1960s. Arriving in Britain in 1963, aged 23, Mota hoped to get a good education and then return to India. However, he found that only his friends were able to help him, not the authorities. Mota needed to find work when he first arrived, but at that time, many people in Britain were not interested in the needs of immigrants.

Mota talks about his early difficulties in finding work and how a lot of the British people he encountered in those days did not like anyone who looked different, ate different food and had different beliefs. Mota wears the traditional Sikh headdress, and he describes how sometimes people would not give him a job because of this. He explains how he has worked hard to overcome these problems and that he now holds an important position in the community where he lives.

Mota describes how he feels that Britain is his home now that he has lived here for so long and has his family here. He also talks of the changes in people's attitudes towards immigrants and ethnic groups that he has noticed since the 1960s. Nowadays, he thinks people really enjoy Indian food and are also better informed about people and cultures from other parts of the world.

Discussing the interview
► Ask the children to tell you where Mota is from and to recall some of the details of his early experiences as an immigrant.

► Talk about Mota's religious beliefs and his traditional clothing. Consider, in a sensitive way, how some people respond to those who wear different or unusual clothes, and why this is.

► Ask the children to recall how Mota managed to find work and to make progress and a new life in Britain.

► Discuss the setbacks that he has had.

► Discuss what he does now, and his feelings about 'home'.

► Think about how different family life is in India compared with Britain.

► List the different ways migration to Britain has changed Mota's life.

► Think about how the arrival of many different groups of people has changed life in Britain.

► Discuss Mota's view of multiculturalism in Britain. Ask the children if they think more change is still needed, and what they would like to see.

Activities
► Ask the children to work in pairs to devise a fresh set of questions that they would like to ask Mota. Review all the questions they have thought of and see if the class can suggest what Mota might have said in response.

► Make a large class collection of books and other resources about the different ethnic backgrounds of people that now live in Britain. Divide the class into groups to research further into aspects of their lives, such as the geographical positions of major communities, their religious beliefs, their traditions and festivals, special foods and so on.

▶ On a large wall map of the world, help the children to mark the places where groups of immigrants have come from since 1948, including people who have arrived, for example, from Ireland, Australia, South Africa, Zimbabwe. Coloured threads could be stretched from their places of origin to Britain.

Notting Hill Carnival in the 1970s

The first carnival in Notting Hill took place in 1965. This is a picture of the 10th carnival, which took place in 1974. The carnival takes place in west London over August bank holiday weekend. Originally, it brought the annual tradition of carnival from the Caribbean to England. It was a continuation of a way of life for the immigrants who had recently come from countries such as Jamaica. It has increasingly brought together all sections of society, from all cultural and ethnic groups, in an opportunity to celebrate together in a truly multicultural event. Unfortunately, due in part to the riots that took place at the carnival in 1976, and because of the activities of the National Front, there has been much increased police presence to ensure the safety of the participants and spectators.

Government efforts to control racial unrest and discrimination have contributed significantly to the harmonious nature of most multicultural communities in Britain today. In 1965, a Race Relations Act made it illegal to refuse people entry to public places because of their race and a Race Relations Board was set up to deal with problems. In 1968, another act made it illegal to refuse people a job because of their race.

Modern Notting Hill Carnival

Notting Hill Carnival has grown to be one of the biggest carnivals in Europe, attracting over a million people of all races and from all over the world. It takes place over the August bank holiday and contains a spectacular array of costumes, music, street stalls, dancing, food and entertainment.

These days, Sunday is 'children's day', and includes all ages. In fact, one of the aims of the carnival is to be all-inclusive. Security fears still persist, but recent carnivals have been happy, successful occasions. The carnival is still an important time for celebration and expression for ethnic groups in Britain. However, it is rapidly being adopted as a national celebration and an important multicultural event, as was the case at the opening of Queen Elizabeth's Golden Jubilee celebrations in 2002.

Discussing the photographs

▶ Look at the photograph of the carnival in 1974. Discuss its size and importance – notice, for example, that a bus is still trying to get along the street amongst the small procession and some people appear to be doing their shopping as normal. Talk about how this illustrates that the carnival may not have been taken very seriously in those days, so everyday life continued around it. Although this is probably only part of it, it does look quite a small affair.

▶ Ask the children to look at the participants and spectators, and discuss their appearance. (Most appear to be Afro-Caribbean.)

▶ Point out the policewoman who is very evident in the scene, and discuss why police presence was so apparent because of the threats from groups opposed to the carnival, such as the National Front.

▶ Talk about how groups grew up who were opposed to immigrants and to the changes they brought – some people had racist attitudes; they may have been joined by people who were afraid that traditional British culture might be lost.

▶ Look at the modern carnival and ask the children what they think the occasion is.

▶ Note how the street is completely clear except for the carnival itself.

▶ Discuss the features of the carnival that they notice first, such as the brightly coloured costumes of the participants, their smiles, the large crowds.

▶ Discuss how the Notting Hill Carnival has now become a much more well-known and loved event and how it is attended by large numbers of people. It is an important event in the British calendar and in British culture.

▶ Ask the children to look at the spectators and discuss their ethnic make-up. (Most appear to be white people.)

▶ Talk about how the carnival has been a strong force in contributing to a truly multicultural society in Britain.

▶ Explain that the carnival theme was important in the Queen's 2002 Golden Jubilee celebrations, and how it made all ethnic groups and cultural backgrounds part of the Jubilee.

Activities

▶ Help the children to locate and label the first Notting Hill Carnival on the timeline on photocopiable page 75 and on a map of Britain or London.

▶ Allow time for the children to work on the computer in pairs to find out further information about aspects of the Notting Hill Carnival, such as where it takes place, its history, the problems the organisers have faced, what the carnival was like in Jamaica, the costumes that are prepared for it. (A website for the 2002 carnival – www.portowebbo.co.uk/nottinghilltv/carnival1.htm#bas – has lots of information, photographs, fun features, advice, comments and useful links.) Encourage the children to add detail to their own timeline of Notting Hill Carnivals.

▶ Provide art materials for the children to make either a large frieze for the classroom walls or their own pictures of the carnival. Use brightly coloured media, such as tissue paper, shiny fabrics and acrylic paints.

Lunar astronaut

In the 1960s, pictures of astronauts (and cosmonauts) became common, both in the printed press and on television. This was particularly true of the astronauts who were the first to go into space or land on the Moon. In 1961, Yuri Gagarin was the first human in space (Valentina Tereshkova was the first woman, in 1963) and Neil Armstrong and his crew were the first men on the Moon, in 1969.

The lunar astronauts' space suits were very bulky because they contained an entire, artificial, life support system to maintain the correct pressure for their bodies, allow them to breath, give insulation against cold, and protect against intense heat, fire and radiation. The suits also contained means of sanitation and numerous electronic devices, especially for communicating with each other, their spaceship and Earth. Their boots were heavily weighted to enable them to walk in a place with lower gravity. The visors in their helmets were gold-tinted and darkened to protect their eyes from UV radiation and glare through the Moon's thinner atmosphere.

Discussing the photograph

▶ See if the children can tell you what this is a photograph of. Explain, if necessary, that it shows one of the first astronauts on the Moon.

▶ Talk about what he wears. Note the significant features of his space suit, for example the huge helmet; the bulky, padded suit that covers his body; the large pack on his back and the mass of monitors and equipment on the front of his suit.

▶ Point out that his hands and feet also have to be completely covered in thick materials, including pressurised gloves. Discuss why this is. (For example, to maintain a safe air pressure, the radiation of outer space would be harmful to a human being – it would burn.)

▶ Discuss what the children think all the electronic equipment is for. (For example, monitoring and maintaining the correct conditions for the body; communicating with the other astronauts and so on.)

▶ Ask a volunteer to identify the flag on the shoulder of the astronaut. Tell the children about the 'space race' between America and the Soviet Union, which received considerable media coverage from the late 1950s. Explain that the first man in space was a Soviet cosmonaut, but the first men on the Moon were American astronauts.

▶ Discuss some of the changes in technology that led to this kind of space travel being possible, for example computer technology and developments in plastic-type materials. Ask for suggestions on how computers would be used during a space flight.

▶ Talk about how amazing the moon landing was at the time, an important world event and astonishing achievement, and that very many people watched the coverage on television.

Activities

▶ On the timeline on photocopiable page 75, help the children to locate and label the dates of the first successful flight into space by Man and the first Moon landing of a manned space flight.

▶ Encourage the children to find out about the space programmes and early journeys into space, for example by the various Vostok and Apollo crews. They could also look at unmanned missions and the animals that were sent into space, such as Laika the dog.

▶ Ask the children to carry out some of their own research into the technological aspects of space suits and the special features that are built into them to enable people to survive outside the Earth's atmosphere.

▶ Help the children to find out about the samples that were brought back from the Moon, known as 'Moon dust', and what has been found out from these. (For example, information about the geological structure of the Moon, its history and so on.)

Space shuttle

The shuttle is the first reusable spacecraft, capable of going on many journeys into outer space. The first model, *Columbia*, made its inaugural orbit of the Earth in 1981. A shuttle is made in three distinct parts: the fuel tank, which is the largest section, the rocket boosters at each side, which fall away back to Earth once the shuttle is launched, and the Orbiter. The Orbiter is the main vehicle, in the centre of the shuttle. This contains the areas where the astronauts live and work. It also contains also the *payload*, or cargo, which usually consists of parts for a space station or a satellite. The Orbiter is the part that returns to Earth like a glider, which the pilot has to land. There are three active shuttle Orbiters at present, called *Discovery*, *Atlantis* and *Endeavor* (the one in this photograph).

Discussing the photograph

▶ Discuss what this photograph shows, or what it reminds the children of, for example an aeroplane, a space rocket.

▶ Establish how it resembles a rocket, for example the rocket boosters firing below what looks similar to a jet plane.

▶ Explain to the children, if necessary, that this is one of the space shuttles, a spacecraft that is able to travel into space and then return to Earth to make further flights. Explain that the shuttle can land on a runway, in a similar way to a conventional aeroplane and then be used again as a space ship. Tell the class about the small fleet of shuttles that are currently in use. Compare this with rocket missions, where the astronauts returned to earth in a small landing capsule, which splashed down in the sea, usually the Pacific Ocean. The astronauts would then be picked up by a naval ship.

▶ Point out the different parts of the shuttle, and explain what happens to the External Tank and Solid Rocket Boosters after launch and ascent.

▶ Ask volunteers to identify the symbols and read the detail on the shuttle and to explain what information this gives us. (Its name, that it is an American craft, run by NASA.)

▶ Talk about why the shuttle was invented and used many times, for example to launch satellites. Discuss how shuttles have made space travel easier and possibly more frequent.

▶ Discuss the meaning of the word *satellite* and discuss the various uses of satellites.

▶ Tell the children about the International Space Station on which crews can live and work for months at a time. Over 16 countries have contributed to the construction and development of the station since 1998.

Activities

▶ Look up the dates of the launches of the different shuttles, for example at http://spaceflight.nasa.gov/shuttle/archives/index.html and present this information to the children in the form of a chart. Challenge volunteers to put the dates onto the timeline on photocopiable page 75.

▶ Provide art media for the children to create their own images and/or models of the shuttle.

▶ Encourage the children to carry out their own research, at school and at home, into the journeys of the shuttles, and to use this information in creating fiction stories to display alongside the artwork.

Hubble Space Telescope

Named after Edwin Powell Hubble, a pioneer of modern space technology, the telescope was built and is operated jointly by NASA and ESA (the European Space Agency). It was launched in 1990, using the space shuttle *Discovery*. It is a space-based observatory, designed to make use of ultraviolet, infrared and visible light to probe further into space than is possible from the Earth's surface. It orbits the Earth every 96 to 97 minutes and is expected to continue working up to a total of 20 years.

Hubble consists of a 2.4 metre telescope, which is constantly being refurbished with new instruments. These include several high-resolution cameras to record what is seen by the telescope. The large panels at each side of the telescope are solar panels, used to provide energy for operating the instruments. British scientists were involved in the development of one of these instruments, the Faint Object Camera.

The United Kingdom has been very successful in keeping in touch with the results of Hubble's findings and has more time for using the telescope than any other country other than the USA. ESA's contribution towards the Hubble Telescope amounted to nearly 600 million euros by 1999.

Discussing the photograph

▶ Ask the children what this object looks like. Have they seen anything like it before? Where do they think it is?

▶ Explain, if necessary, that it is the Hubble Space Telescope, which works in space, and orbits the Earth regularly, like a communications satellite.

▶ Ask them what they think the different parts of the object are. (The central cylindrical section is the telescope and the two side sections are solar panels.)

▶ Discuss how solar panels work and talk about why the telescope needs them to provide power for its instruments.

▶ Ask the children why they think scientists decided that a telescope was needed in space and discuss the advantages of a space telescope over a terrestrial one. (Explain what *terrestrial* means if necessary.)

▶ Ask the children when they normally hear the terms *satellite* and *terrestrial* and discuss how we can now receive television pictures in both ways.

▶ Talk about the large number of satellites that are in outer space, and the work that they do, for example in transmitting television pictures and for telecommunications in general, such as telephones and the Internet.

Activities

▶ Help the children to locate and label the launching of the Hubble telescope into space on the timeline on photocopiable page 75.

▶ Suggest the children look at www.nasa.gov/forkids. Here they can find out further information about all aspects of technology in space. Divide the class into groups to work on different aspects of this technology, such as the shuttles, the spacestation, the Hubble Telescope and the different satellites that are in space. Create a class book for them to collect all their findings together. More information on Hubble can be found at http://hubblesite.org.

▶ From their findings, ask the children to make labelled pictures for display of all the satellites they have found out about or the images Hubble has provided.

▶ Help the children to research the work of Edwin Hubble.

Interview: How life has changed since 1948

This interview was held with Jack Hogbin, who lived as a child in a rural area of Dover in the years before 1948. Jack talks about the many changes he has seen in Britain since that time. He feels that there have been enormous changes that have affected the lives of ordinary people. These have included different types of heating in homes, new domestic appliances, such as electric cookers and fridges, new forms of travel and a much wider availability of foods throughout the year. Before all these changes took place, Jack remembers life being much harder.

Leisure activities have also changed since Jack was a child. While modern children tend to spend a lot of their leisure time watching television, in his day, they went to the cinema or played in the street.

Jack thinks that the main changes he has seen have been in the general levels of prosperity of ordinary people and also the developments in communication. These things, he feels have made the lives of ordinary people much more comfortable, varied and exciting.

Discussing the interview

▶ Discuss what the decade from 1940 is known as. (The 1940s.)

▶ Discuss what Jack remembers as being different about the homes of ordinary people in the years before 1948.

▶ Ask what sorts of things children did for entertainment at that time.

▶ See if anyone can recall how cooking was done, and what cookers were like.

▶ Think about where most people got their food before 1948, especially if they lived in the country. Ask for suggestions on what people grew for themselves in their gardens.

▶ See who can remember what Jack said about things that were not available then. For example, what foods did people never have? Discuss why this was. For example, technology had not reached a level where chilled and frozen foods were widely available, so produce was eaten when in season, foods from far distant places were less available because transport was slower and fruit, for example, could not be stored for long enough. Ask the children to suggest other foods that would not have been available for similar reasons.

▶ Ask the children to recall the changes that Jack thinks are the most important, and discuss the reasons he gives for these changes.

Activities

▶ Give the children a blank timeline marked in years throughout the 1940s. Challenge them to carry out their own research and put on their timeline an event for each year, for example the introduction of the NHS as an important nationwide change in healthcare (see photocopiable page 80). As well as important events and the dates of significant people, they could talk to family members and put on the birthdays for anyone born in this period.

▶ Using the video clip and the extract from the transcript on photocopiable page 79 in conjunction with the pictures on the CD, ask the children to find images of the things Jack describes in the interview. Tell them to label them and make a class display about the 1940s.

▶ If appropriate, ask the children to interview grandparents and compare their thoughts on changes with those of Jack. Ask them to include mention of the background the interviewee came from – rural/urban, poor/wealthy.

NOTES ON THE PHOTOCOPIABLE PAGES

Word cards

PAGES 72–4

The word cards build on vocabulary suggested by the QCA, and introduce words related to:

▶ settlement, such as *population, emigration, immigration*

▶ aspects of society, such as *industry, work, leisure, transport, media, fashion*

▶ change, such as *same as, because, cause, effect, reasons*.

Encourage the children to think of other appropriate words to add to those provided, in order to build up a word bank for the theme of Britain since 1948. They could include words encountered in their discussions and research, such as *Indian, Caribbean, Commonwealth*, in relation to discoveries about the parts of the world that people came from. They could also use the cards in displays and in writing sentences to record what they have learned. They should also use the word cards as support in descriptive, factual and creative work and in writing discussions and arguments.

Activities

▶ Once you have made copies of the word cards, they could be used for word games and spelling games, and for children to invent their own games.

▶ Make displays of aspects of migration and use the word cards to label them.

▶ Encourage the children to use the words in stories and non-fiction writing as often as possible.

▶ Ask the children to use key words in summarising new learning about Britain since 1948.

▶ Make wordsearches and crossword puzzles for the children to complete using specific sets of words related to the topic, such as words to do with different aspects of social change.

▶ Make cloze procedure sheets omitting key words from the text. Encourage the children to write the words without support.

▶ Devise '20 questions' and 'Hangman' games based on the word cards.

Photograph © Photodisc

Timeline of Britain since 1948

PAGE 75

This timeline can be used to introduce children to the notion of chronology over a certain span of time, in this case, the period in British history since 1948. It can also be used to illustrate the variety of terms used to talk about time and chronology, in particular the word *decade*. The information the timeline contains focuses mainly on key events in British history since 1948, and various economic and technological changes that affected society. It also includes references to important legislation on race relations and the death penalty, about both of which there was considerable debate at the time. The timeline helps to show the kinds of social change, such as the concerns over issues of equality in society, that characterised this period in history.

This timeline could be used alongside photographs and illustrations about Britain since 1948, to give children some visual representation of chronological sequence and of changes and events that took place. It could be adapted for the classroom in the form of a long string stretched across the classroom, representing the distance in time covered by the period. Alternatively, it could be adapted to create a large wall frieze to which other information could be added by the children about different figures, such as Margaret Thatcher or Princess Diana. Further pictures and dates could be added as the topic progresses.

The kind of timeline shown here can also be useful at the end of a topic for checking children's success in grasping ideas of sequence, chronology, change and understanding of the use of dates. This particular timeline will be useful also in discussions about the reasons for and effects of key legislation and economic developments. Children could be asked to create their own version of a late-20th-century timeline or be given a blank outline to complete by positioning events in the correct order and pictures in the appropriate places.

Discussing the timeline

▶ At the beginning of the topic, ask the children what they think this timeline shows.
▶ Clarify what the dates on the timeline mean. Explain that this line with dates and pictures represents the passing of time.
▶ Talk about the key events during British history since 1948, and add more labels and events as appropriate.
▶ Point out the wars that took place during the period, and discuss how many conflicts Britain has been involved in in recent years, such as the Gulf War and the Falklands War.
▶ Use the accounts and tables on photocopiable pages 76–9 and the pictures provided on the CD to illustrate the discussion about the timeline.

Activities

▶ Make a class timeline, using the timeline on photocopiable page 75 as an example. Ask the children to put on, in the appropriate places, any other photographs, illustrations or portraits from the period they find or create themselves.
▶ Read other accounts from the history of Britain since 1948, including some of those included on the timeline.
▶ Give the children a blank timeline with some key dates included and ask them to draw or paste relevant pictures onto it in the right places.

Population change

PAGES 76–7

These pages focus on two different kinds of information about changes brought about by immigration into Britain in this period. The first table, on photocopiable page 76, shows how the population of the UK increased steadily in the second half of the 20th century, and how immigration began to increase greatly in the last decade shown. It also shows how the death rate within the UK has begun to approach the same level as the birth rate. The second table, on photocopiable page 77, is useful for showing the places of birth of the population, and how immigration from the 'New Commonwealth' countries of India, Pakistan, Bangladesh and the Caribbean has increased greatly since 1961. It needs to be noted, however, that the figures for 1961 only cover England and Wales, while the others cover the whole of Britain, so they are not exactly comparable.

An explanation of how to read the data to help children begin to interpret the content of the first table has been provided, but it is assumed that the children will have some understanding of how to interpret the data by the time they progress to studying the second table.

Discussing the tables

▶ Look at the table on photocopiable page 76 first. Help the children to scan the data in the table and then read through the notes explaining what the contents of the rows and columns show.

▶ If the children have had little prior experience of reading and interpreting data of this kind, read through and explain each column carefully.

▶ Note how the period is divided into decades (column 1) and the second column shows the total UK population (in thousands) at the start of each ten-year span, and how the last column shows the comparative number at the end of that time.

▶ Ask the children to comment on these figures. Prompt them with questions such as *What has happened to the population since 1951? How much has it increased?*

▶ Ask the children to explain what columns 3 and 4 show and the changes they indicate. An important point to note is how the number of births has decreased, and how the number of deaths has changed very little.

▶ Ask the children how, therefore, they can account for an overall increase in the population.

▶ Look at the column of net immigration, and explain what it shows. Point out the minus figures, explaining how these show that more people left the country at this time than entered it.

▶ Next, look at the second table with the whole class. By now the children should be more able to read this type of chart and understand the meaning of the figures.

▶ Encourage volunteers to explain what each row and column shows.

▶ Ask individuals to expand on the changes shown by the figures. (For example, the greatest increase in immigration has been from the New Commonwealth countries.)

▶ Discuss why this might have happened. (For example, they were invited to work in this country; there may not have been enough jobs for them in their places of birth.)

▶ Mention that some of these immigrants were probably children. Discuss what it must have been like for children to move to a new country. What would have been different?

Activities

▶ Divide the class into five groups and allocate to each group one column from columns 2 to 6 on the table on photocopiable page 76. Ask them to write what their column shows about population change. If possible, let the children use the computer suite to write their sentences, then collate them, displaying the whole text on a screen or interactive whiteboard. Work with the whole class to write some concluding sentences about what one column shows if compared with another. (For example, notice how births have declined, but population has continued to grow as a result of immigration.)

▶ Challenge more able children to carry out further research about the information in the first table to establish why more people were leaving the country in the 1960s and 1970s than were arriving. They could try to think of some possible reasons beforehand and see if their ideas prove correct. (For example, there may have been fewer jobs in Britain at that time; recent immigrants had lived in Britain for some time and had moved on elsewhere or returned to their native countries.)

▶ Challenge children to discover why more people began to arrive from the New Commonwealth countries since the 1980s. (For example, as Britain's wealth increased people saw greater opportunities for improving their lives, chances to set up small businesses, more jobs with higher salaries than in their home countries, better education and prospects for their children.)

Immigration accounts

PAGE 78

These extracts are from interviews with two Jamaican immigrants, describing their experiences.

John Richards arrived from Jamaica in the 1960s. He describes what it was like to be sent to a strange place – 'the shelter' where early immigrants were housed if they had nowhere to stay at first. The account explains how large the shelter was, how strange it seemed to live underground, and how organisations would come to recruit the new arrivals to jobs they had to offer.

The text may read strangely in places for two reasons; firstly, John's speech contains some Jamaican dialect, which makes some of his expressions different from Standard English; secondly, the text does not read like a 'normal' written text, as it is a transcription of speech.

The interview with Tryphena Anderson gives some background on what happened in Jamaica as more people prepared to leave for Britain. It reveals the strong, mixed emotions emigrants felt and how their friends and relatives collected all they could to help them on their way, including food and money. What comes across clearly is the mixture of emotions felt by those leaving their home.

Again, the text is unusual to read at times, because of its transcription from speech and the dialect used.

Discussing the text

▶ Read through the first extract with the children and ask them what kind of text they think it is. Who wrote it and why?

▶ Explain that this and the following piece are both short extracts form interviews, and that these interviews, with many others, were published in a book.

▶ Discuss what was happening to John Richards. For example, where has he come from? Where has he arrived?

▶ Establish where Clapham is and how he got there.

▶ Explain to the children what the shelters were – deep underground shelters for people to go to during the bombing in the Second World War, built to accommodate large numbers.

▶ Ask the children why they think the immigrants were sent to this place.

▶ Read through the second extract and discuss the type of text this is.

▶ Talk about what is happening to Tryphena, and why she feel as she does. Why does she feel both happy and sad?

▶ Ask volunteers to explain what the friends and families did to help those who were leaving.

▶ Talk about how nowadays, many people leave their home countries for many different reasons. Ask the children what reasons these might be. (For example, to find jobs or a better way of life; to be with others in their families; to escape from a dangerous situation.)

▶ Discuss the sound of both extracts when read aloud, and explain to the children how people from Jamaica, and other parts of the world, speak English as their first language, but in a slightly different way, with an accent and using dialect. Explain that when speech is written down, it is not the same as other forms of written English.

Activities

▶ Watch the interview with Mota Singh on the CD and compare his experiences with those given on the photocopiable page.

▶ Challenge the children to use the tables on photocopiable pages 76 and 77, adding to them a list of all the different immigrant groups they can find. Then ask them to write two or three sentences about these groups from their personal research. For example, what countries have they come from? What is it like in their places of birth? What languages and religions are there in their places of birth?

▶ Challenge the children to use these extracts to make up a story on the life of an immigrant.

Changes I have seen since I was a child   PAGE 79

This text reproduces part of the interview with Jack Hogbin provided on the CD. The extract includes some of the key changes that Jack has noticed, particularly domestic ones, which will be meaningful to young children. Jack was a child during the 1940s and has been asked what he thought the main changes have been since that time. He talks about the domestic changes he thinks are significant because they have affected everyone's lives. He picks out home heating technology and labour-saving domestic appliances in particular, explaining how very different life is now compared with the hard work needed to run a home in the 1940s.

Like 'Immigration accounts', above, the text is different from typical written English, having been transcribed from conversation, and the children will need to be made aware of this fact.

Discussing the text

▶ Read the text with the children and discuss how the text has been created. Explain the meaning of the word *transcript*.

▶ Ask the children to recall which people would have had central heating, and how most people would have heated their homes.

▶ Discuss the difficulties caused by having to light coal fires, for example for children or for Jack's parents.

▶ Talk about the ways in which modern central heating works. Consider that many families have central heating in their home nowadays, and the effect this has had on people's lives.

▶ Explain what Jack means by *black lead*, and why things made from iron had to be black-leaded to prevent them rusting and to keep them clean and shiny.
▶ Think of some of the domestic appliances that have been invented since the 1940s, such as toasters, electric kettles, food processors and microwave ovens. Talk about how the jobs done by these would have been done in the 1940s.
▶ Ask the children to think of what effects these developments have had on individuals and on home life in general. (For example, mothers can now go out to work more easily; we can have clean clothes more often.)

Activities

▶ Review the video with the children and, working with the whole class in a shared writing session, make notes of the other major changes that Jack identifies.
▶ Work with the children to devise a schedule of interview questions and then set them the task of interviewing an older family member or friend about significant changes they have seen since their early childhood. Advise the children that they will need to make brief notes or tape record what is said and then tell the rest of the class what they have discovered.
▶ Set the children the task of writing to individuals, requesting an interview. Encourage them to use proper letter-writing conventions.

The National Health Service
PAGE 80

This text gives a brief background to the setting up of the NHS and describes the kind of opposition that was faced. Finally overcoming these, the service began in 1948, accompanied by a mood of public enthusiasm. The comments from those involved in the debate illustrate the two opposing views and show the ideals held by those in favour of its introduction.

It is not an easy text to use, since it contains a mixture of narrative and comments extracted from writing and speeches. The children will need to realise that the text is made up of several kinds of information, taken from different sources. There are terms, titles, names and ideas that are likely to be unfamiliar to the children, and these will need explanation. The allusion to the system practised in Germany will have been particularly significant so soon after the Second World War, and discussion about why this was used as an argument will encourage the children to put themselves in the position of people at that time.

Discussing the text

▶ Read through the text with the children and question them about the events that it describes. For example, what is being proposed? Who are the people in favour of it?
▶ Discuss the thoughts of the people against the idea, who they were and why they were opposed to it.
▶ Talk about the kind of health care that was available before 1948 – private care that had to be paid for and so was not available to everyone. Discuss what happened to people who were not well off. They had to save money in case they were ill; they would often go to the chemist for advice rather than the doctor; some would try out their own remedies at home.
▶ Ask the children why those who supported the service decided to wait until the war was over before beginning to set it up.
▶ Ask the children to identify some of the groups who opposed the idea, and explain the meaning of *Conservative*, and *Medical Association*.
▶ Discuss why the BMA member used a comparison with Germany as part of the argument against the idea. Get the children to imagine how most people in Britain would have felt about German ideas so soon after the war.

Activities

▶ Challenge the children, working in pairs, to write speeches about the case for a new national health service. They could build on the statements provided in the text.
▶ Set the children the task of writing letters to the press, explaining that this is one way of showing support or opposition to an important issue. Tell the children to state the case against a health service for the whole country. They will need to think who would have written such letters, such as Conservative politicians, or doctors who were against the idea.
▶ Organise a class debate about the issues involved, telling half to be against the plan and the others in favour of it. At the end of the debate, conduct an independent vote to find out the overall view.

industry

work

leisure

transport

media

fashion

diet

communication

Settlement word cards

population
emigration
immigration
settle
former colonies
movement of people
refugees
culture

Change word cards

different from
same as
because
cause
effect
reasons
results
consequence

Timeline of Britain since 1948

End of clothes rationing — **1948**	
	1949 — First jet airliner flight
End of petrol rationing — **1950**	
	1951 — Festival of Britain
Britain develops atomic bomb — **1952**	
Hillary climbs Everest — **1953**	Coronation of Queen Elizabeth II
	1954 — End of food rationing
ITV begins broadcasting — **1955**	
	1956
	1957 — Jodrell Bank radio telescope completed
	1958
M1 motorway opened — **1959**	
	1960
	1961 — Hovercraft with skirt developed
The Beatles release first album and number 1 singles	1961
	1963 — Beeching makes railway closures
BBC2 begins broadcasting — **1964**	
	1965 — Death penalty abolished
First British colour TV broadcasts — **1966**	England wins the football World Cup
	1967
	1968 — Race Relations Act passed
Concorde's first flight — **1969**	
	1970
Currency decimalised — **1971**	
	1972
	1973 — The UK joins the EEC
	1974
Sex Discrimination Act passed — **1975**	
	1976
	1977 — Elizabeth II's Silver Jubilee
	1978
Margaret Thatcher becomes first female British PM — **1979**	
	1980
	1981 — Wedding of Charles and Diana
Falklands War — **1982**	UK unemployment reaches 3 million
	1983
Miners strike begins — **1984**	
	1985 — Live Aid
Chernobyl nuclear accident — **1986**	
	1987
	1988
	1989
	1990
	1991 — Gulf War
	1992
	1993
Channel Tunnel opens — **1994**	
	1995
	1996
	1997 China regains Hong Kong
Princess Diana dies — **1997**	
	1998 Scottish Parliament and Welsh Assembly opened
Good Friday Agreement made in Northern Ireland — **1999**	
	2000 September 11 terrorist attack in New York
Foot and mouth outbreak — **2001**	
Princess Margaret and Queen Mother die — **2002**	Elizabeth II's Golden Jubilee
	2003 War in Iraq

Population change (1)

Population change in the UK 1951–2000
Figures are in thousands

1	2	3	4	5	6
Period	UK population at start of period	Births	Deaths	Net international migration	UK population at end of period
1951–61	50 290	840	596	8	52 807
1961–71	52 807	961	640	−9	55 928
1971–81	55 928	742	667	−33	56 352
1981–91	56 352	756	654	44	57 561
1991–00	57 814	699	601	117	59 756

▶ Column 1 shows the start and end dates of each period of time. The rows next to these dates include all the figures collected for that period of time.

▶ Column 2 shows the total number of people in the United Kingdom at the beginning of the ten-year period shown.

▶ Column 3 shows the average annual number of births that took place during that ten-year period.

▶ Column 4 shows the average annual number of deaths that took place during that ten-year period.

▶ Column 5 shows the net international migration to the UK that took place during that ten-year period. This is the total number of immigrants minus the total number of emigrants. A minus figure shows that more people left the UK than came in during that period.

▶ Column 6 shows the total number of people in the population of the United Kingdom at the end of the ten-year period shown.

Population change (2)

Country of birth of people in England and Wales/ Great Britain

Figures are in thousands

Country of birth	1961	1971	1981	1991
United Kingdom	43642	50670	50197	51114
Republic of Ireland	644	709	607	502
EU (not UK & RoI)	337	–	408	531
New Commonwealth	360	699	924	1013
– Caribbean	172	237	295	265
– India	157	322	392	409
– Bangladesh	–	–	49	105
– Pakistan	31	140	188	234
Old Commonwealth	137	189	170	245
Total outside UK	1420	3088	3360	3775
Total population	44447	53979	53557	54889
	(England & Wales)	(Great Britain)	(Great Britain)	(Great Britain)

Source: UK Census country of birth tables

Note: EU is European Union.
RoI is Republic of Ireland.
Bangladesh came into existence in 1971.
Previously it had been part of Pakistan.

Immigration accounts

New arrivals from Jamaica aboard the *Windrush* were given a place to stay in the deep shelters on Clapham Common. Among them were law students, dockers and people who wanted to be chemists and scientists. They were given a public welcome to Lambeth by the Mayor. This extract is from an interview with one of them, John Richards.

> I came to Tilbury and then we're coming along on the coach, because they brought a coach and took us to Clapham... What was strange is when we have to go down, because we'd never been down in the earth like that, something strange. But then, after a while, you get used to it. It wasn't bad, you know, because that place is a very big place, because one evening we was walking, I never reach the end of it. We was walking along, and we walk and walk and walk, and there was bed two sides, until we get to the end and turn back. But it wasn't bad. The things were clean and we get food to eat down there, and things like that. But I've been in worse places than that. I don't know if it was two hundred or a hundred and fifty, there was quite a few of us down there. But then gradually we dispersed, because some of them, the Army come down and recruit some, the RAF come down and recruit some, everybody got different places. The coal mines, people come down and recruit some at the time, things like that.

Many others followed the first immigrants to Britain in the next few years. This extract is from an interview with Tryphena Anderson, who left her homeland at the age of nineteen.

> My friend from school, she came down from the north side of the island and stayed with us. And everybody come, they bring you gifts, gifts of money. And then they do a lot of cooking, things you can eat on the way. And they bring large handkerchiefs, because they're going to cry, you know. And I was glad, I was sad, and it was an excruciating pain. You're going away. And everybody gets in this truck. You're in the front, they're trying to make you happy, and they were sad, because these are the people that you know. So, we drove down. It wasn't like one of those excursions we used to go on, where you're singing, 'Riding along on the crest of the waves'. There was no waves. It was all the people wanting to hug you, touch you.
>
> Then we get to Kingston to the airport. The tears start to flow, and then I had to move away, and I don't think I've ever dragged my feet like I dragged them that day.

From *Windrush: the Irresistible Rise of Multi-racial Britain* by Mike Phillips & Trevor Phillips

Changes I have seen since I was a child

One of the things that is very different is that many homes now have central heating. [When I was a child] only the very rich had central heating and most of us had coal fires. Now central heating heats every room in the house, but a coal fire only heated one room, so you spent most of your life in one room, which was usually the kitchen, and the front room was only for very special occasions.

This meant also that when you did your homework you certainly either had to do it in the bedroom, where it was freezing cold, or your parents had to be very helpful to you and let you do it in the kitchen while it was quiet, and that wasn't very easy.

And coal fires made a big difference. My dad used to have to get up very early in the morning and make the coal and the wood and the newspaper ready to light the fire so that when everybody else came down, that room was warm. The other difference was that the food was cooked on a stove which also had coal in it, and this meant that a kettle had to boil over a coal fire, and Mum had to go and what was called 'black lead' the oven, which meant that the oven was made of iron and it had to have this 'black lead' paste smoothed over it from time to time. So that was one very big difference.

Another big difference was that there was no washing machine, no fridges, there were no dishwashers, nothing like that at all. Which meant that washing up was all done by hand and all the clothes. We have clean clothes every day now, but not in those days, because no one could have managed all the washing that was required.

The National Health Service

The first step towards setting up the National Health Service was taken in 1942, when William Beveridge, a lawyer, economist and former civil-servant, published proposals for setting up a health service once the Second World War was over. It was to be free (funded through taxation) and easily accessible to everyone everywhere.

Aneurin Bevan, Minister of Health in the Labour Government after the war, took on the job of setting it up as part of a plan of welfare reform. He faced strong opposition from many sides, including the Conservative Party and the doctors' professional organisation, the British Medical Association.

Despite continued opposition from the Conservatives and from many doctors, the National Health Bill was passed by Parliament in 1946, and took effect in 1948. In the end, reluctant doctors accepted the public mood of enthusiasm for the service, and began to join it.

Here are a few examples of comments made from different sides in the argument about the National Health Service:

The essence of the satisfactory health service is that the rich and the poor are treated alike, that poverty is not a disability and wealth is not an advantage.

Aneurin Bevan

The National Health Service is the biggest step forward that has ever been proposed in this House of Commons, in an attempt to keep the people of this country healthy when they are well and to deal with them kindly when they are ill.

Bessie Braddock (MP for Liverpool Exchange)

I have examined the Bill (to introduce a health service) and it looks like the kind of system practised in Germany.

From *The British Medical Journal*